Releasing the
Revival Flood

Additional Books by Dr. Frizzell

Available Church and Region-wide Conferences

Going Deeper With God Weekend

Developing Mountain-Moving Prayer,
and Intimacy with God

Journey to Holiness and Power

Church and Association-wide Revivals,
and Solemn Assemblies

Transformed Relationships, Healed Families,
and United Churches

Holiness and Power in Christian Leaders

Developing Powerful Prayer Meetings,
and Prayer Ministries

Powerful Prayer Meetings and
Evangelistic Prayer Ministries

Powerful Marriage and Family Prayer

Biblical and Historic Patterns of Spiritual Awakening

Escaping the Trap of Dead Religion

For information concerning conferences or resources
contact Dr. Frizzell:

Baptist General Convention of Oklahoma
3800 N. May Ave., Oklahoma City, OK 73112-6506
phone: 405.942.3800 e-mail: gfrizzell@bgco.org

Releasing the Revival Flood

Overcoming Relationship Barriers to Personal & Churchwide Renewal

Dr. Gregory R. Frizzell

Releasing the Revival Flood – Overcoming Relationship Barriers to Personal and Churchwide Renewal
ISBN 1-930285-22-1

Published by The Master Design
  in cooperation with Master Design Ministries
    PO Box 569
    Union City, TN 38281-0569
    bookinfo@masterdesign.org
    www.masterdesign.org

Additional copies of this and other books by Dr. Frizzell may
be ordered from:

Baptist General Convention of Oklahoma
3800 N. May Ave., Oklahoma City, OK 73112-6506
phone: 405.942.3800 e-mail: gfrizzell@bgco.org

Printed by Bethany Press International in the USA.

JJ

Contents

Author's Preface
It's All About Relationships!

Words can hardly express my excitement at the growing signs of awakening in God's remnant! Without question, more and more saints are beginning to seek God in deeper prayer and repentance. While God may yet have to judge America and shake a sleeping Church, at last His small remnant is stirring. This spiritual stirring is especially encouraging because God sends revival through just such a remnant and God finishes what He starts! (Philippians 1:6) In view of God's activity, Releasing the Revival Flood seeks to address a final unaddressed barrier to the long-awaited flood.

While we can gladly report a rising prayer movement, there is at least one crucial element yet to show much progress. That crucial element is deep loving unity and koinonia fellowship among believers! In fact, we not only have not seen much progress, we have witnessed a disturbing collapse of love and unity. One thing is certain — if we are to see revival, believers must reject division and return to loving unity.

Loving unity is so utterly critical that Jesus places it as one of only two Great Commandments. (Matthew 22:37-38) Jesus even tied our evangelistic witness to the strength of love and unity among believers. (John 13:34-35;21:17) The issue is so vital that Scripture even states that no one can be unkind and unforgiving, and still be right with God. Thus, according to the Bible, it really is "all about relationships." But in spite of God's strong commands about unity, a tragic trend has developed. Church conflict, division, and tension have risen to shocking levels! Though long-term research data is not exhaustive, surveys leave no doubt that church tension, splits, and staff firings are at devastating highs. Virtually nothing shames Christ's name more nor hinders His Spirit more than church and denominational division. But let every reader take hope — God can heal the most divided believers and churches!

Removing Relational Barriers

Yes, even in today's troubling crisis of disunity, there are early signs of hope. More and more believers are weary of all the fighting and tension. Increasingly they are asking why there is such division and tension in our churches. While there are many reasons, certainly one is a lack of strong, specific resources on this vital subject. Though there are thousands of sermons, books, and courses on evangelism, discipleship, and nearly every other subject, serious focus on churchwide unity has badly lagged behind. When relational barriers are mostly ignored, all other ministries are bound to lack full power.

While the New Testament continually addresses relational patterns in churches, modern congregations have been largely silent. The tragic result is an epidemic of churches paralyzed by damaging patterns of tension and disunity. No wonder we are seeing low conversion rates, exhausted pastors and a rash of church splits. Yet when we address relationship patterns biblically, God brings glorious change in places seemingly hopeless!

We Can Recapture the Missing Key!

God's Word assures every reader that there is hope for even the most battle-torn church or family. No doubt, I am writing to some who wonder if their churches could ever see loving unity and revival. Some readers may so struggle with personal weariness, anger, or bitterness that they can hardly imagine a flood of love and power. Dear friend, please believe God can and will remove your relationship barriers.

It is especially encouraging to note that great revivals can indeed come to the most seemingly unlikely people and places. Thank God, His grace is greater than our greatest weakness! From deep personal experience of serious illness and inheriting a pastorate in a grave, long-term battle, I assure you God can bring loving unity and revival anywhere! Whether you are in a strong church (that hasn't quite moved into revival) or a desperately dry, divided congregation, this book is designed to help you recognize and remove your barriers to sweeping revival. While it will certainly take repentance, the results will be worth it a million times over.

Increasingly, saints are saying "We are ready for a revival of love and oneness!" Releasing the Revival Flood is dedicated to removing the barriers and restoring closeness with God. But more than being a book you read, this tool is a journey you experience with God. Throughout Section Two, we will examine the major patterns by which Satan divides God's people. In every step of the journey, God's grace offers forgiveness and glorious transformation to all who truly want to grow.

As you read, there may be times when God speaks so specifically, you will think someone has been spying on your church. If that happens, please know it is almost certainly God speaking directly to your heart. (1 Corinthians 14:15) None of the patterns in this book came from particular churches or people. As I thoroughly researched and prayed, I simply asked this specific question: "God, what is most breaking your heart and preventing revival in today's churches?" I must confess I had no idea where that prayer would lead me. In fact, I really did not set out to write this particular book. Yet God soon made it clear, the patterns in this book are what most prevent the revival flood. But praise be unto God — these patterns can be reversed!

My friend, in every step of this journey, remember God's incredible grace and love. While no believer or church is anywhere near perfect, we can identify the main barriers and discover glorious new life. Let us settle for nothing less than the full glory of God's manifest presence. Most of all, may we never forget, revival is not an "it" but rather a He — Jesus Christ Himself! Dear saints, let us at last return to the vital understanding that "loving God means loving each other." To Him be all glory and praise forever!

Toward the Next Great Awakening
Your Brother and Friend,

Gregory R. Frizzell

Section One
Preparing for a Flood
of God's Presence!

Introduction

Have you ever experienced the mighty power of a flooding river? Even if you have not, you have surely witnessed gripping news coverage of such events. When a major flood occurs, all normal activities cease and lives change forever. In the realm of weather, we all know the catastrophic life-altering effects of such an event. But now I ask you to consider the possibility of an entirely different kind of flood. A flood that would bring miraculous and wonderful changes to your life, family, church and nation. Consider an event so huge that everything about your life, church and world changes forever. My friend, I am referring to something incredibly real and entirely possible. I am speaking of a sweeping revival flood of the presence and power of God Himself! (Isaiah 44:3; Acts 2:1-2)

A Mighty Flood is Truly Possible
Barriers Can Be Removed!

It is vital to understand such mighty floods of God's presence have indeed happened many times and can surely happen again. Consider God's incredible imagery describing mighty outpourings of His Spirit. In Isaiah 44:3, God refers to sending forth His Spirit like "floods of water on dry ground and upon the thirsty." Jesus described His Spirit as "*rivers* of living water flowing from our hearts." The unique Greek word *patamos* used here for rivers, implies a continual gushing torrent or flood of God's Spirit!

In Acts 2:2, God's manifest presence was the "sudden sound of a rushing, mighty wind and a fire that filled the disciples." Even our English word for "dynamite" comes from Jesus' words describing the power to flow through His followers. (Acts 1:8) Dear reader, I want you to believe God is both ready and able to flood your life and church with an explosion of His presence. Though God's mighty flood in your circumstances may not come overnight, it *will come* if you are willing to let Him remove your barriers! In fact, some of the most incredible transformations come to the most battered people and troubled churches. So how about it, friend? Are you thirsty for a move of God? One thing is certain — no repentant person or church is too far gone for God's mighty touch!

As I write these words, my heart fills with an inexpressible excitement. At last there are growing signs that God is up to something not seen since the last Great Awakening. All across the land, we see evidence of growing spiritual hunger, increasing prayer and at last deepening repentance. While admittedly, this rising tide is only a very small percentage, it is growing! Let us take hope in the fact that God sends revival floods through the small percentage, *not* the lukewarm majority. Dear reader, please believe God desires to flood your life, family and church with an explosion of His presence. No matter how long you may have struggled, we serve the all-powerful, merciful God Who finishes what He starts. (Philippians 1:6) There is no question that God has started calling His people to a whole new level of closeness!

Yet you may well be asking, "Where are the signs of this potential revival flood?" After all, the dark clouds of moral collapse and spiritual decay are exploding on every hand. But remember an encouraging truth — *revivals usually explode in times of darkness and trial, not comfort and ease*. After all, floods come to *dry* ground and great light dawns in times of deepest *darkness*. On that score one thing is obvious, it is getting gloriously dark! In fact, it is clear we are already under some level of judgment. It is also true that God may have to send greater judgments to fully break and turn us to Himself. But even if God has to send far greater chastisements, His ultimate desire for believers is redemption, healing and restoration. He will likely do whatever it takes to hear the burdened prayers of millions He has called to prayer. And yes, even if it must begin with judgment, a revival flood would be well worth whatever is required to see it!

But Why Should You Seek a Revival Flood?

Without question, seeking a revival flood should be the heart and passion of every saved person. Yet let us be very clear — our primary goal is *not* just seeking a revival flood, it is seeking the *Reviver Himself.* At its heart, a revival flood is simply a far greater love, surrender and closeness to God Himself! And when you truly experience God in intimacy and depth, you experience life itself. Indeed, no amount of money, fame, success or blessings could ever begin to compare with simply knowing God in tremendous depth and power. "*Now this is eternal life: that they may know you, the only true God, and Jesus Christ, whom You have sent.*" (John 17:3) "*The thief comes only to steal and to kill and to destroy:*

I have come that they may have life, and have it to the full." (John 10:10)

But well you may ask, "What would a revival flood really look like?" The historic descriptions are truly mind boggling! Consider some awesome facts. If America saw another Great Awakening, between *twenty and thirty million* new converts would explode into churches within two to four years! Based on historic patterns, a church of one hundred in attendance will baptize between fifty and one hundred persons in a single year. A church of a thousand, would likely baptize between five hundred and a thousand persons in a single year. Even quarreling, divided churches in tough surroundings would soon see miraculous growth and unity! In revival, the modern scourge of dry, bickering churches would turn into a flood of glorious unity and love. Burned out, defeated leaders would receive glorious healing and renewal. And best of all, God's name would receive great glory.

Revival Brings About Transformed Families and Churches

A revival flood would not only radically change churches, but society as well. Ratios of crime and immorality would immediately plummet. Patterns of serious family breakup would dramatically improve. By the millions, broken lives and relationships would be mended bringing great glory to God. Social improvements and missions would explode many fold. In a great flood of revival, evangelism and global harvests explode through the roof!

Dear reader, if all this sounds like a fairytale, I assure you it is not! These descriptions and percentages are exactly what God has done many times in history. It may sound impossible to us, because America has not witnessed such a move of God since the mid-1800's. Yet there is good news. Our God has not changed and He *can* do it again! (Hebrews 13:8) In fact, several places in the world are seeing mighty moves of God right now. Just because we have not *seen* a flood, does not mean we will not.

Since we know God *can* send revival, the question is, "Why hasn't He?" The answer is two fold. First, most believers and churches have not met the conditions in prayer and repentance. Second, relational barriers of anger and bickering are seriously blocking His Spirit in most families and churches. But thank God, there *is* an answer and relational barriers *can* be addressed by renewed prayer and obedience.

Revival Brings an Explosion of Intimacy and Power with God

We now turn our attention to the greatest of all blessing that comes from a revival flood. Surely the greatest blessing is the incredible new closeness with God Himself. For believers who often felt distant and found it hard to hear God's voice, His voice suddenly becomes clearer than those of even spouses and best friends! For those who struggle with areas of spiritual bondage or unanswered prayer, God's power begins to flow like a river. (John 7:38) Impossible mountains begin to move and long awaited answers at last arrive. Churches and ministers long dry and weary, suddenly burst forth with new life. While a revival flood certainly does not remove all suffering, God's grace becomes so real we tend not to care. In fact, revived believers often literally rejoice in their persecutions and trials! (2 Corinthians 12:9)

Dear saint, if you are among the millions who struggle to achieve a strong prayer life or intimacy with God, *please take hope*. Spiritual power is not out of reach and God definitely desires to help you remove your barriers. But even beyond personal blessings and closeness with God, there is another purpose greater than all other. That purpose is simply pleasing God and glorifying His name! Indeed, true revival is all about *Him*, not us.

Revival Unites Believers and Glorifies God
Christian Love and Unity —
The Ultimate Way to Glorify God

Without question, the single greatest reason for seeking a revival flood involves the primary purpose of our existence. And what is that primary purpose? It is to know, love, glorify and obey God by loving one another. Friends, when we learn to seek first His kingdom and His righteousness, we find life itself! *"But seek you first His kingdom and His righteousness, and all these things will be given to you."* (Matthew 6:33) *"Whoever loses his life for Me and for the gospel will save it."* (Mark 8:35) Indeed life is all about "knowing Him," surrendering to Jesus and walking humbly with our God. (John 17:3) Jesus pulled it all together in His two Great Commandments. *"Love the Lord your God with all your heart and with all your soul and with all your mind. This is the first and greatest commandment. And the second is like it, Love your neighbor as yourself."* (Matthew 22:37-39)

Absolutely tied to our purpose of knowing and loving God is the commitment to loving unity with fellow believers. (Matthew 22:37-38; John 13:34-35;17:21) It is crucial for believers to realize Jesus' two Great Commandments are inseparably linked! In other words, no one can truly love God and yet be unkind or bitter to fellow Christians. In Matthew 5:23 and 6:14-15, Jesus said disunity and bitterness utterly block fellowship and blessing from Him. Never has our nation seen such devastating disintegration of church and family relationships. What we have witnessed in family structure is no longer merely a decline, it is an unmitigated *collapse!* More than any other factors, relational anger and unforgiveness are now likely the biggest barriers to a modern day revival flood!

Church Conflict and Family Disunity — "Preeminent" Barriers to Revival

In light of today's pandemic immorality and compromise, it may even sound strange to call disunity a "preeminent" revival hindrance. Yet surveys clearly tell us that church conflict, division and lack of love are even more prevalent than out-right immorality (at least in the church). And according to Jesus, relationship sins are actually even more spiritually offensive then some of the more outward sins of the flesh. (Matthew 5:23;6:14; John 13:34-35) It is incredibly significant that every New Testament book contains strong commands for fervent love and unity among believers. No other single issue receives greater focus in God's Word. The point is simple — God is extremely serious about strong love and unity among Christians!

Yet for all the seriousness of relational love and church unity, congregations hear astoundingly little emphasis or direct teaching on this subject. Unfortunately, what is shared is usually very general and vague. Detailed specific descriptions like those in this resource are seriously neglected. Yet this is exactly the kind of specific biblical teaching required for God to bring deep conviction and healing to damaged relationships! Throughout all of revival history, restored relational oneness has often been a significant factor in sweeping revivals. This tool is specifically designed to help return churches and families to the long missing element of healing damaged relationships.

Church Bickering and Disunity
"The Devil's Favorite Game —
The Church's Greatest Shame"

There is something unspeakably ugly about disunity and fighting in churches. Not only do these patterns utterly quench God's Spirit, they devastate our witness and power in evangelism. (John 13:34-35) Without question, anger and disunity break the heart of the Savior who literally died to make us one. When believers cannot get along in reasonable peace, Christ's name is shamed and lives are irreparably damaged. Jesus said the world would be *drawn* to Him *by our love*, but they are also *repulsed* by our anger and bickering! (John 17:21) No wonder the enemy spends so much time and energy inflaming bitter battles and disagreements between believers.

In fact in today's church, there is a growing scenario as predictable as clockwork. Throughout twenty years of pastoring, doing conferences, and research, I must have heard the following agonized statement a thousand times. *"Just when our church was really showing progress, we had a major explosion of angry blowups and divisions — it just seemed to come out of nowhere.*" It is no surprise this pattern is especially common when a church is starting to see many people saved and great progress in missions and ministry.

In order to hinder or stop churches, the devil constantly seeks to exploit issues and divide believers. (1 Peter 5:8) It is so predictable that we must be ready with powerful tools for both prevention and correction. Paul confirmed this sentiment when he wrote that we should not be "ignorant of Satan's devices lest he gain the advantage." (2 Corinthians 2:11, KJV) *Releasing the Revival Flood* is designed to uncover the devil's "relational devices" in believers and churches.

Uncovering the Enemy's Relationship Tactics
"We Wrestle Not Against Flesh and Blood"
(Ephesians 6:10-18)

As one would expect, the devil works most often under a cover of darkness. Current studies reveal several relationship patterns that are tragically common in many congregations. Again and again, these same relational barriers are stopping revival in thousands of churches. Though these patterns are clearly wrong, they are issues difficult to clearly address in sermons or conflict resolution programs. At their heart, these are "spiritual battles" and "heart issues" not merely personality or psychological conflicts. Most of these patterns will not be solved by human conflict resolution techniques alone. While such techniques are certainly very important, they must be combined with the spiritual cleansing principles outlined in God's Word.

While we all know certain evil relational patterns are present in church, they are much like the "*elephant in the room*" that few address directly or effectively. Make no mistake — until God's people are fully discipled and enlightened on these specific devices of the enemy, revival will be an impossible dream for most churches and families. No matter how many evangelism, discipleship or prayer efforts we embrace, the Holy Spirit will remain seriously quenched in an atmosphere of underlying anger and bickering.

In this book, we seek to help congregations discern their relationship barriers to sweeping revival. Many saints are caught in these patterns without knowing God's Word on what is really happening. This book is filled with Scripture because of Jesus' powerful promise — "*Then you will know the truth, and the truth will set you free.*" (John 8:32) Until believers and churches come to recognize God's truth about Satan's divisive relationship tactics, these devastating patterns will surely continue.

In the coming pages, congregations will embrace a journey of deep cleansing and transformation. As we see several areas needing change, let us remember God's power is sufficient! Thank God there is hope for even the most troubled church and weakest Christian. How good to know we are accepted and under grace even in our struggles. It is truly glorious to know that we are "accepted in the Beloved" though our knees may be skinned from many falls and struggles.

Because this tool deals with some deep, long-standing issues, I feel it is important for believers to keep several key truths in perceptive. Readers should be aware, this book is not "casual reading." As many churches read through this study, some will sense they have struggles in almost every area. For this reason, it is vital for every reader to remember one glorious truth. *God's grace is bigger than all our weaknesses and He still works in very imperfect churches (which includes us all).* Let no reader become discouraged when he sees several areas needing change. Our God does not expect perfection, just honest steps to start addressing the issues He reveals. Before you begin this journey, it is important to consider the following foundational truths.

How to Encounter God Through This Journey
"Key Perspectives Before You Begin"

(1) *Let this journey point you straight to Jesus' grace and forgiveness, not to condemnation or discouragement.* (Romans 8:1; 1 John 1:9) As you read through the potential revival barriers, some points will bring awareness and conviction of sins previously unrealized. Please understand that God is convicting only to bless and transform your life, not to hurt or condemn you. Above all, do not let the devil turn God's conviction into condemnation, discouragement or despair. Though we all have many areas needing work, God still views us as *"righteous through Jesus' blood."* As you begin to confess and forsake your sins, God will surely bless in ways you cannot even imagine. Though it likely will not happen overnight, stay with the process — you really *can* experience a flood of His power and presence!

(2) *As God reveals spiritual barriers, immediately confess all sin and embrace concrete steps of repentance.* (Proverbs 28:13) It is vitally important both to confess and forsake the sins! Strongly resist the fleshly tendency to become angry or defensive about your areas of need. Above all, do not try to excuse or rationalize your failures. It is

11

important to remember that God's specific conviction raises your accountability to repent many-fold. It is essential that we not put God off or only partially repent. God strongly warns against such blatant abuse of His grace. (Hebrews 10:26-31)

If you or the church has offended someone, get wise council and by all means go and ask forgiveness in the spirit of Matthew 5:23. Conversely if there are people you have not truly forgiven "from the heart," you must admit it and truly forgive them now! Dear reader, this is not so much a book of lessons to be "studied" as it is clear Scriptures to be "obeyed."

(3) *As God reveals areas of needed change, by faith appropriate Christ's life as your victory.* (Romans 6:6,14; Galatians 2:20; Colossians 2:6) Do not try to gain victory in your own strength or legalistic efforts. Just as we are saved and declared righteous by faith, we also daily grow and change by faith. From the start to the finish of our walk as His children, He accepts us in the righteousness of His Son. (Ephesians 1:6) Above all remember, you *do* have the ability to repent and change by the Christ Who lives within you!

(4) *Learn to focus on relational unity as a lifestyle, not merely a study course to do and lay aside.* (1 Peter 5:8) The issues in this resource are not areas we read once and lay aside. At one reading God may speak in certain areas while at a later reading He will reveal something totally different. This biblical journey is designed for repeated periodic use as God's Spirit guides. Because Satan so constantly seeks to damage relationships, churches should probably embrace a thorough relational checkup at least every two to three years.

(5) *Periodically use this tool for "prevention" of potential spiritual barriers as well as "addressing" those currently active.* (Psalm 119:11; 2 Corinthians 10:3-5) In essence, this resource is a practical tool for discipling believers in healthy church unity. Studies show very few believers (or pastors) have had clear instruction in these specific issues. In a fair number of cases, believers simply do not realize these relational patterns are as wrong as the Scriptures indicate. It is crucial that we regularly teach on these relational patterns that hinder revival. When they are clearly and regularly taught using Scriptures, God's Spirit will do the rest!

(6) *Use this tool as a powerful Bible-based weapon for spiritual warfare.* (Ephesians 6:1-13; 2 Corinthians 10:3-5; James 4:7-8) Today a major problem is that many spiritual warfare tools deal mostly with principles and neglect to unmask the devil's specific tactics. While it is certainly essential to understand our theological foundations of victory, it is the devil's daily tactics that are destroying believers and churches. It is most disturbing that students can still go all the way through seminary and barely get a word about relationship dynamics that are eating churches and ministers alive. Unfortunately, the patterns described in this resource are where most churches really live. For this reason, it is vital that we begin to teach the spiritual dynamics of relationship wars in our churches! After all, it is the enemy we do not see that usually gets us. Use this tool as a practical, Bible-based strategy for helping our members fully recognize and reject the devil's tactics in their churches and families.

(7) *This tool is designed equally for pastors, church leaders and laypeople.* (Romans 2:11; 14:10-13) While some of these barriers rest more on the shoulders of leaders, others relate more to laypeople. This tool is not designed to target any group more than the other. It is also true that in any one of these issues, we as pastors and denominational leaders can be just as ensnared as laypeople. Every person should pray through this tool with your eyes on what God is saying to *you*, not what you think He might need to say to someone else! Above all, no one should use this book as a weapon to beat someone else over the head. As we all pray through this material privately, we must trust God to do His work in ourselves and others. As we thoroughly expose churches to His Word about relational barriers, the Holy Spirit will do the rest.

(8) *This resource is about "refocusing" church priorities as well as "removing" spiritual barriers.* (Matthew 6:33;21:13;28:16-18) Though mostly about relationships, this tool also has key elements of adjusting church strategies in ways necessary for revival. Without question, a huge hindrance to revival is the neglect of key kingdom patterns by which God works. *Examples include abandoning prayer meetings or being self focused rather than kingdom-focused in church visions.* Our purpose is not only allowing God to *remove* patterns of sinful barriers but to *add* patterns of kingdom-focus. Because of this focus, some points deal more with leadership and those who decide strategic vision. Please be prepared to make whatever adjustments are needed in church priorities and vision.

(9) *Do not let the enemy convince you that your church is so problem ridden it is hopeless.* (Romans 8:1; Ephesians 2:8-10) Without question, one of the most encouraging books in the all the Bible is Paul's first letter to the Corinthians. The epistle is especially encouraging because their particular church had virtually every possible relationship problem, yet God still loved and used them! As your read through this tool of transformation, God will likely reveal several areas needing growth and change. Be encouraged that our God is a wise and merciful Father who blesses and delivers us by grace, not because we deserve it (which none of us do). Each reader should work on the major areas God reveals and trust His grace to cover the rest. Even the most mature among us will always be a work in progress. While we must take seriously the things God reveals, we should not fall victim to condemnation or discouragement.

(10) *Not all conflict is bad and is often a normal part of growing together as Christians.* (1 Corinthians 12-14; Colossians 3:8-17) It is certainly true that no two people agree or have the same tastes in all things. Even husbands and wives have real differences yet they still share incredible unity. Indeed, a most vital part of Christian growth is church members working through ways we disagree without becoming angry, condemning or disrespectful. It is further true that mature saints can learn to disagree on non-essentials without compromising essentials. No reader should think that revival requires church members to continually sit around in white robes and sing "kumbaya." Again, the grace of our God is a wonderful thing! Thank God, He still works in our midst though we all have many areas needing growth.

(11) *Use this tool as a scriptural mirror or plumb line to help provide a clear vision of who we are to be as Christ's Church.* (Amos 7:7-8; James 1:23-24) This tool is designed to hold up the biblical mirror of specific relationship characteristics of revived, New Testament churches. It also helps us clearly see the specific relational patterns hindering the revival flood. To help us see the point, let's consider the simple physical analogy of looking in a mirror. If we never looked in a mirror, something about our appearance could be badly out of place yet we would never know it. Furthermore, if we looked in a mirror that was oily or distorted, our self image would be vague and unreliable.

Releasing the Revival Flood provides a clear image of specific patterns that hinder the flood of God's Spirit. While clear sight can at first be painful, the "godly sorrow" and "specific conviction" are generally necessary for revival floods. But let us never fear our loving Father. He prunes us for our good and wounds only to heal. May God use this tool to remove the barriers and release the mighty flood of His Spirit.

(12) *Along with other new member materials, consider giving this tool to adults who join your church.* (Psalm 119:11; John 8:32). When someone joins, it is an excellent time to stress the importance your church places on New Testament unity. While you would certainly not suggest your church is anywhere near perfect, you would at least tell them of your church's commitment to love and unity. Today we must face the fact that a certain percentage of people change churches for precisely the reasons outlined in this book. They either actively

caused some of these conditions or they are trying to escape them. Either way, the truths in this book are vital for them to read.

When it comes to church conflict, remember two axioms. (a) "It is much easier to address disunity and anger patterns *before* you are in the middle of a battle." (b) "When it comes to church conflict, 'an ounce of *prevention* is worth a pound of *cure!*'" Having new members read this book could be a practical way to prevent or minimize problems before they can occur.

(13) *Be aware revival that floods require conviction that produces deep and thorough repentance.* (2 Corinthians 6:14-7:1; Hebrews 12:14) Today's Church has a disturbing tendency to try and avoid deep conviction. Furthermore, when sin is dealt with, it is often in general and vague terms. For this reason, believers seldom experience either the depth or specific type of conviction that brings real change. Friends, if we have any chance of seeing a sweeping revival flood, there must be a return to just the type of clear descriptions contained in this book. Dear leaders, let us not be afraid to share spiritual meat with saints who have too long heard milk regarding the subjects in this book. Let us not fear Holy Spirit-produced conviction as it leads to true repentance, healing and joy. In truth, a return to "godly sorrow" over sin is our only hope of the revival flood!

(14) *Let us all be careful to reject any tendency to judge or look down on those involved in relational conflicts.* (Galatians 6:1-4; Ephesians 4:29-32; 1 Peter 4:8) One thing is for sure — none of us are completely without sin when it

comes to insensitivity toward others. Even when we cannot help but note obvious patterns of error in some, we should ever remember, "*There go I but by the grace of God.*" Dear readers, we must love and show patience to erring believers. We are never more like God than when we love those who do not love us. While there will surely be times we must squarely address their sins of speech, we must do so in love and humility. By that spirit, God sends enormous healing and reconciliation. In that spirit, He brings the revival flood!

A Final Word to My Readers

Releasing the Revival Flood is actually a pilot version of a larger, more user-friendly resource soon to be released. Though all are certainly invited to read these pages, this pilot version is mostly designed for pastors, staff and church leaders. The final version, entitled *Loving God Means Loving Each Other*, contains study and prayer guides for very easy use by individuals, small groups and whole congregations. It also contains much more emphasis on grace-based processes for actually overcoming churchwide relationship barriers to revival.

The new resource has even more emphasis on encouragement, grace and practical steps for change. It also contains several more topics dealing with issues besides relationship barriers to revival. The final version contains virtually every major area that hinders God's Spirit from moving in power: *Careless Committees and Flesh Guided Councils; Buried Bitterness; False Forgiveness and Shallow Reconciliation; Immorality and Compromise; Key Sins of Omission; Overcoming False*

Views of Grace; Developing Leaders of Holy Boldness and Victory Over Lukewarmness. Without question, God is calling us to an incredible journey of cleansing and change. And thank God, it is a journey of grace and life, not condemnation and fear. My friend, are you ready for a glorious turning point? God surely desires to give you the greatest turning point of all—closeness with Himself!

God's Glorious Invitation to All

In James 4:8-10. God issues an awesome invitation to every reader: "*Come near to God and He will come near to you. Wash your hands, you sinners, and purify your hearts, you double-minded. Grieve, mourn and wail. Change your laughter to mourning and your joy to gloom. Humble yourselves before the Lord, and He will lift you up.*" God not only promises to "draw near," He tells us exactly how to approach Him. We come to Him by "cleansing our hands and purifying our hearts." That is exactly what will happen as you journey through Section Two. And you already know the outcome. He is going to remove your barriers and release the revival flood!

As you embrace this journey with God, I have two simple suggestions. (1) *Each time you prepare to read a portion of this book, pause and ask God to speak to your heart.* Ask Him to help you avoid the fleshly reaction of anger or defensiveness when He convicts of an area for change. When God convicts about areas of sin, we generally have one of two reactions. People who are lost or backslidden typically react with anger, defensiveness or rationalizations to excuse their sins. Those with hearts after God, immediately become broken, contrite

19

and repentant. They soon experience glorious forgiveness, healing and blessing!

(2) *If at any point in this journey you have the slightest doubt about your salvation, immediately pray through Appendix B and God will guide you to perfect peace!* Even now, if you know you have been struggling with doubt, go to that section and allow God to give you perfect peace. There is no reason for you to live another day in doubt and defeat. Let this journey be your life-changing turning point. Let it be the beginning of your own revival flood!

Section Two
Removing the Barriers —
Releasing the Flood!

Addressing the Twenty-Four
Most Common Hindrances

As a writer, I am more and more convinced there is only one opinion that counts and it sure isn't mine. There is surely nothing as powerful as the plain and simple Word of God in Scripture. This cleansing journey is drawn straight from Scripture at every point. Because God's Word is so central, I believe it important to have each reader carefully pray through a few key selected Scriptures as we begin the journey. The following Scriptures are only a few that relate directly to the subject we address. A much fuller listing is found in Appendix A which I ask every reader to examine. Please carefully and prayerfully read these direct words of God to your heart.

God's Word to Loving Fellowship and Unity
"Recognizing Christ's All-Important Command!"

Proverbs 6:16 – "*These six things doth the Lord hate: yea, seven are an abomination unto Him: A proud look, a lying tongue, and hands that shed innocent blood, an heart that deviseth wicked imaginations, feet that be swift in running to mischief, a false witness that speaketh lies, and **he that soweth discord among brethren**.*"

Matthew 5:23-24;6:14-15 – "*Therefore if thou bring thy gift* to the altar, and there rememberest that thy brother hath ought against thee: leave there thy gift before the altar, and go thy way; first be reconciled to thy brother, and then come and offer thy gift...For if you forgive men their trespasses, your heavenly Father will also forgive you: But if you forgive not men their trespasses, neither will your Father forgive your trespasses."

John 13:34-35;17:20-22 – "*A new commandment I give unto you, that you love one another; as I have loved you, that you also love one another. By this shall all men know that you are My disciples if you have love one to another...Neither pray I for these alone, but for them also which shall believe on Me through their word; That they all may be one as thou, Father, art in Me, and I in Thee, that they also may be one in Us; that the world may believe that Thou hast sent Me. And the glory which Thou gavest Me I have given them; that they may be one, even as We are one.*"

1 Corinthians 1:10;3:1-3 – "*Now I beseech you, brethren, by the name of our Lord Jesus Christ, that you all speak the same thing, and that there be no divisions among you; but that you be perfectly joined together in the same mind and in the same judgment...And I, brethren, could not speak unto you as unto spiritual, but as unto carnal, even as unto babes in Christ. I have fed you with milk, and not with meat: for hitherto you were not able to bear it, neither yet now are you able. For you are yet carnal: for whereas there is among you envying, and strife, and divisions, are you not carnal, and walk as men?*"

Ephesians 4:3 – "*With all lowliness and meekness and longsuffering, forbearing one another in love; Endeavoring to keep the unity of the Spirit in the bond of peace.*"

Ephesians 4:29-32 – "*Do not let any unwholesome talk come out of your mouths, but only what is helpful for building others up according to their needs, that it may benefit those who listen. And do not grieve the Holy Spirit of God, with whom you were sealed for the day of redemption. Get rid of all bitterness, rage and anger, brawling and slander, along with every form of malice. Be kind and compassionate to one another, forgiving each other, just as in Christ God forgave you.*"

Titus 3:10-11 – "*A man that is a slanderer after the first and second admonition reject; knowing that he that is such is subverted, and sinneth, being condemned of himself.*"

James 4:11-12;5:9 – "*Speak not evil one of another, brethren. He that speaketh evil of his brother, and judgeth his brother, speaketh evil of the law, and judgeth the law: but if thou judge the law, thou art not a doer of the law, but a judge. There is one lawgiver, who is able to save and to destroy: who art thou that judgest another?…Grumble not one against another, brethren, lest you be condemned; behold, the judge standeth before the door.*"

1 Peter 4:8-9 – "*And above all things have fervent love among yourselves: for love shall cover the multitude of sins. Use hospitality one to another without grudging.*"

1 John 3:10-15 – "*In this the children of God are manifest, and the children of the devil: whosoever doeth not righteousness is not of God, neither he that loves not his brother. For this is the message that you heard from the beginning, that we should love one another…We know that we have passed from death unto life, because we love the brethren. He that loves not his brother abides in death. Whosoever hates his brother is a murderer: and you know that no murderer hath eternal life abiding in him.*"

1 John 4:7-8 – *"Beloved, let us love one another: for love is of God; and every one that loveth is born of God, and knoweth God. He that loveth not knoweth not God; for God is love."*

The Biblical Commands of Loving Respect for Christian Leaders

Psalm 105:15 – *"Touch not mine anointed, and do my prophets no harm."*

1 Corinthians 1:10 – *"I appeal to you, brothers, in the name of our Lord Jesus Christ, that all of you agree with one another so that there may be no divisions among you and that you may be perfectly united in mind and thought."*

Ephesians 4:2-3 – *"Be completely humble and gentle; be patient, bearing with one another in love. Endeavoring to keep the unity of the Spirit in the bond of peace."*

1 Thessalonians 5:12-13 – *"And we beseech you, brethren, recognize them which labor among you, and are over you in the Lord, and admonish you: and to esteem them very highly in love for their work's sake. And be at peace among yourselves."*

1 Timothy 5:17 – *"Let the elders that rule well be counted worthy of double honor, especially they who labor in the word and doctrine."*

Hebrews 13:17 – *"Obey them that have the rule over you, and submit yourselves: for they watch for your souls, as they that must give an account, that they may do it with joy, and not with grief; for that is unprofitable for you."*

(All verses above are from the King James Version)

In this section, we identify and describe twenty-four of the most common revival hindrances that come from within congregations. While a few of the descriptive titles may seem a bit lighthearted, be assured God finds nothing humorous in these conditions. As you read each one, ask God to show whether you or your church have any of these significant patterns. Most of all, ask God whether you are in any way part of these devastating patterns. God is ready to cleanse and heal your life, please let Him!

Dear reader, as you embrace this journey it is crucial to be completely honest with yourself and with God. Remember, God convicts because He loves you and wants to set you free! If you heed His voice, great blessing and mercy will shower your life and church. Yet if you ignore His words, lost blessing and serious chastisement must eventually follow. It is my fervent prayer that every reader will choose life and mercy, not chastisement and forfeited blessing. As you prepare to read the following pages, pause and ask God to speak clearly to your heart. Listen for His voice and immediately confess every sin, forsake any wrong and make all restitution to which He leads. And know beyond doubt, He will set you free!

Pattern One
Angry Attitudes, Buried Bitterness, and False Forgiveness

"Loving God Means Loving Each Other!"
(Matthew 6:14-15;18:21-35; Mark 11:25; Luke 6:37;
John 13:34-35;17:21-23; 1 Corinthians 13:1-8; Ephesians 4:29-32)

In light of today's shocking church battles, surely among the most devastating of all revival hindrances is unforgiveness and critical unloving attitudes among believers. In a day of rampant immorality, it may even sound strange to say relational bitterness and unkindness are the biggest hindrances. Yet surveys leave no doubt that relationship barriers are even far more common than immorality. According to Scripture, there is little worse in God's eyes than believers harboring bitterness or unkindness toward other believers! Dear reader, if that statement sounds exaggerated, please carefully read the specific references under this section's heading. The Bible is clear that nothing displeases God more or quenches spiritual power more than underlying bitterness and unkindness to others!

God literally considers angry, divisive attitudes and behaviors an abomination. (Proverbs 6:16b) Paul even includes unkind, abusive speech in exactly the same category as idolatry and gross immorality. (1 Corinthians 5:11) When believers are negative, critical and unkind God is profoundly displeased. If believers barely speak and avoid one another, the Holy Spirit is seriously grieved and quenched. (Ephesians 4:30: 1 Thessalonians 5:19) To ignore rifts between fellow believers is to make a mockery of Christ's death and purpose — to make us one in His love!

Yet tragically, most modern believers more or less ignore this issue. In fact, many view anger and damaged relationships as somewhat normal and unavoidable. There is no area in which the devil has more tragically pulled the wool over the eyes of God's children. Many saints simply do not treat forgiveness, kindness and unity with real seriousness. Many think as long as they are avoiding physical immorality and outward aggression, their spiritual bases are covered. Nothing could be further from the truth! Jesus said the "main thing" (alongside evangelism) is fervent, heart-felt love toward God and loving forgiveness to others.

Forgiveness and Loving-kindness Among Believers — God's Essential Focus!

While the Great Commission is obviously the "main thing" of what we *do*, the two Great Commandments are the main things of what we *are*. When our *hearts* are right with God and each other, evangelism and missions will explode through the roof. Yet to try and pray or conduct evangelism without deep love and forgiveness assures little power and small success. But even worse, our unforgiveness and anger absolutely breaks Jesus' heart and shames His name before a lost world. After all, He literally gave His life that we would love one another and be united as one!

In John 13:34-35 and 17:21, Jesus flatly states that Christian love and unity are absolutely central to our evangelistic witness. Today we certainly see the results of neglecting these central commands — dry divided churches, broken families, little prayer power and lost joy! Thank God, there is a remedy to today's deadly patterns of anger, bitterness and disunity. My friend, no matter how long these may have described your life or church, you can be miraculously changed!

Unforgiveness Toward *Others* — The Sin That Imprisons *You*

It is most significant that Paul described several of the works of the flesh as wrong attitudes and words toward others! In most cases, we develop underlying anger and bitter attitudes because we have not "from the heart" forgiven others. Often we "say" we have forgiven or "let something go" when we really have not. This is why Jesus added that all-important phrase, we must forgive "*from the heart.*" (Matthew 18:35) Make no mistake — when we don't truly forgive, our prayers are blocked, and we lose God's power. But even worse, we tread on the Son of God. (Hebrews 10:26-31)

One thing is certain — in this life we have all been wronged, and will probably be wronged again. That is why Jesus said if we are to be His followers, we must forgive others "as He has forgiven us." And how does He forgive us? He forgives with a rich, "unconditional" love. Even if people will not admit their wrong or ask our forgiveness, we can and must still take the "position" of forgiving them in Christ. This attitude protects us from the devastating poison of internalized bitterness.

Forgiveness does not mean we minimize what others have done or "feel" warm and gushy about the situation of the wrongs. It is wonderful to realize that true forgiveness is a "choice" and is not dependent on our feelings. We forgive by trusting Christ for the power to forgive and overcome the anger that would otherwise control us. Yes as humans, we will certainly feel the pain of a wrong. But through Jesus, we can daily "choose" to forgive and not be imprisoned by anger. When we begin to make the consistent choice to forgive, healing and deliverance can then begin in our emotions. Yet, until we genuinely choose forgiveness, we grieve God's Spirit and remain trapped in our pain. But friends, there is good news — the One who literally forgave as He hung on a cross lives within us and can forgive through us. Our part is to daily make the sincere "choice" to forgive and show kindness, His power will do the rest!

Counseling Center Miracles and Church Transformations

When doing an internship in a professional counseling center and nearly two decades of pastoring, I noticed a glorious key to transformed lives. We often asked people to prayerfully read Matthew 6:14-15;18:21-35 and Ephesians 4:29-32. They were then urged to take a few days and prayerfully list every person against whom they harbored the slightest bitterness or anger. At first, they usually said they could only think of one or two they needed to forgive. Yet, as they asked God and waited, they soon realized there were many others against whom they had buried bitterness.

In reliance on Christ, we asked them to choose forgiveness and take daily steps to embrace an attitude to literally pray for the person who had hurt them. While with some it certainly took some time and several steps, the miracles were indescribable! Their joy returned, God was glorified and the Holy Spirit began a mighty new work in hearts, families and churches. But there was always one huge key — they had to become *honest* about their unforgiveness, *stop justifying* it and *choose* to daily forgive through Christ's life within. My friend, you must do the same thing. And by God's grace, you can!

Renouncing Our Angry Attitudes
"Agreeing to Disagree Agreeably"

Closely related to the hindrance of bitterness, is believers who have an angry, touchy or critical spirit. Again we see in God's Word, there is little more displeasing to God or hindering to the Holy Spirit. *Furthermore, a huge percentage of church conflict and division can be traced to members with angry, critical attitudes.* While as believers we certainly do not agree on everything, we can and must commit to "disagree agreeably." Friends, if we simply resolve to treat each other with kindness and respect, it is amazing how many battles and conflicts quickly melt away. It is astounding how many battles would never occur in the first place! Dear friend, there is more good news to report — some believers and churches are getting so weary of the battle, they are truly ready to change. And by God's grace, they are changing!

But again, let there be no mistake as to what God is telling His Church. It is an *abomination* for believers to continue in divisive anger and unkindness toward one another! (Proverbs 6:16d) God's heart is profoundly grieved when some members will not speak to one another (especially Church leaders not speaking to other leaders!) It is deeply offensive to God when some members go out of their way to avoid having to be around other members. Unkind words and attitudes are the very opposite of God's purpose for His people. If such patterns are allowed to persist, even our very worship and prayers are an empty ritual.

Based on Scripture, how could we think God is anything but profoundly grieved in any church where this is widespread and continuous? These angry attitudes and so-called "little rifts" are typically even more hindering to God's Spirit than more outward sins of the flesh. Oh dear reader, *please* be honest with yourself and honest with God about these matters. If you will be honest and take the clear steps revealed in Scripture, God will surely touch your life, family and church! (John 6:37) And remember — He doesn't require perfection, just willingness to be honest, to stop making excuses and to take some basic steps of repentance. Neither does it require everyone in the church being willing to change. If only a few will begin to obey, it is astounding what God can do to eventually touch the others. His grace is certainly greater than the sin of those who are willing to stop making excuses and take basic steps to obey.

We Can All Change!
(Romans 6:14; Philippians 4:13)

No doubt many reading these pages are very weary, wounded and war-torn. You may struggle with bitterness and unforgiveness because you have experienced some truly horrible things in your life. My friend, God's compassion and grace especially goes out to you. With others, for whatever reason you have long had a harsh temper and quick trigger. Despite your circumstances, God's grace is sufficient to help you now become a kind and forgiving person. I have seen it happen in some of the most angry, negative people!

But it is essential that we all take this very seriously. It is no accident we began our look at revival hindrances with the issues of unforgiveness and angry unloving attitudes. *Virtually all the other battles in churches stem from these foundational sins.* As you work through the rest of this book, virtually all the other barriers come from these roots. Yet be encouraged — God is stronger than our strongest sins! Dear reader, go before God and consider whether He is already leading you to some key steps of confession and repentance. Above all, start with simply embracing a truly loving, forgiving attitude. You and your church will never be the same!

Potential Steps to Take

1) Fully confess and ask God's forgiveness for patterns of unforgiveness, anger or unkindness toward others. Take significant time and let Him truly *search* your heart. (Psalm 138:23-24) Do not rush this process or minimize your sins. Do not in any way justify or rationalize your sins. **You must fully confess and forsake them.** (Proverbs 28:13; 1 John 1:9)

2) Ask God to help you fully forgive "from the heart" all who have wronged you. Be sure to go way back into the past and be very specific. I strongly encourage finding a godly counselor or prayer partner to help with the process. Read Matthew 18:15 and go to people if that applies to your situation. By all means purchase and read the book *The PeaceMaker* by Ken Sande. It will provide very complete biblical guidance for virtually all relational issues.

3) If you know you have been unkind toward specific

people, fully confess and forsake this most grievous sin to God. As God leads, you must go in love to those you have offended; humbly ask their forgiveness and make whatever restitution may be needed. (Matthew 5:23-24)

4) Claim God's total forgiveness and forgive yourself! My friend, we are all sinners and you must do with your failures what God does — He removes them as far as the east from the west! He chooses to remember them no more. (Hebrews 8:12)

A New Day Will Dawn!

Your miraculous change of heart will almost certainly be a process, so do not be discouraged if you do not see mountain-moving miracles overnight. Daily resolve to make loving-kindness and forgiveness your number one priority. Trust God and repent through every up and down in your journey. And know for certain — you are "accepted" in the Beloved and His grace is sufficient for you to become incredibly loving, kind and forgiving. (Ephesians 1:6; Philippians 4:13) Above all, let us embrace love and forgiveness for God's glory and His kingdom. Only in this way do we live as sons and daughters of God.

I close this crucial first section with a final suggestion. If unkindness and bitterness have been a significant pattern in your life, I strongly urge you to read Appendix B before proceeding. Again, many people struggle with God not being real in their life and thus lack assurance of their salvation. When God is not real to us, anger and bitterness tend to be far more of a problem. It is truly hard to make progress until the assurance issue is effectively solved. Let God give you perfect assurance. He definitely wants to become far more real in your daily life. Best of all, when God is real in your daily life, love and forgiveness will fill your heart!

Pictures of Grace and Hope

Over many years of pastoring and professional counseling, I have witnessed incredible miracles of change in people's lives. Some of the most angry and bitter people have become loving and kind. People with long track records of hot tempers have become gentle and patient. Believers who have feuded for years, at last dropped their pride and humbly asked forgiveness. Their healing and transformation have been astounding!

When believers confess underlying anger and bitterness, the effect on their church is simply awesome. People whose attitudes have long hindered revival, soon become the very agents for a sweeping revival flood. When separated saints forgive one another God's presence rushes in like a river. Dear believer, do you hear God's voice to your own heart? Could revival hinge upon you forgiving and asking forgiveness of someone else? Absolutely!

Pattern Two
Victory Over Gossip,
Innuendo and Slander

(Matthew 18:15; Ephesians 4:29-32; Titus 3:10-11)

There is absolutely no doubt that patterns of church gossip, division and verbal slander are at crisis levels in today's Church. The same must be said of many denominations and organizations. Yet, as we prepare to examine today's damaging patterns of gossip and slander, it is vital to remember one glorious truth. Our Lord convicts to point us to Himself in grace and hope, *not* to ourselves in condemnation and despair! Dear reader, if God reveals new areas of sin in your own heart, do not be overwhelmed. Even if you see significant patterns that badly need change, please know that our Lord brings "godly sorrow" to produce repentance and blessing. Let us rejoice in the fact that God's grace is greater than the greatest sins of anyone willing to repent. May each of us read this section with hearts ready to hear God's voice and change by His wonderful grace. And praise God, we *can* change!

As I have researched factors hindering revival in today's churches, it is clear that gossip, slander and division have become epidemic. It is also true that sins of speech have taken ever more vicious forms. Unfortunately, some of these patterns are very subtle and people can become ensnared without clear awareness it is even happening. One of the most common and deceptive is a subtle misuse of the so-called "prayer concern." While legitimate prayer requests are always important, some regularly drift into patterns of turning prayer concerns into a very damaging form of gossip. People with this tendency frequently spread gossip and slander under the guise of sharing a "prayer burden." It seems they are always needing to share some "concern" that really ends up being much more a discussion of salacious rumors than actual prayer.

Some people are lightening quick to spread gossip, slander or problems under the guise of "concern for the church." All the while they completely miss the fact God clearly says we are to first take issues or problems to someone privately and *not* to anyone else! (Matthew 18:15) Yet people with this pattern do just about everything but go to someone privately. Or if they finally do go to someone, they've usually gone to everyone else first. And after they've gone, they tell everyone else every word of the conversation. (Does this sound familiar?) People ensnared in this sin also ignore the fact that God strongly condemns repeating rumors and tales in any form. (Proverbs 11:13)

The Neglected End-All Cure for Gossip

Ninety-five percent of gossip and slander would immediately cease if believers simply obeyed the crystal clear command of Matthew 18:15-17. "*If your brother sins against you, go and show him his fault just **between the two of you**. If he listens to you, you have won your brother. But if he will not hear thee, then take with thee one or two more, that in the mouth of two or three witnesses every word may be established. And if he shall neglect to hear them, tell it unto the church; but if he neglect to hear the church, let him be unto thee as an heathen man and a publican.*" These commands of Christ leave absolutely no doubt as to how we are to address grievances or concerns between believers. Scores of other Scriptures also clearly forbid gossip, speculation and all forms of rumor-mongering. One thing is certain—following God's command puts an immediate stop to virtually all forms of talking about people behind their back!

Because the pattern of Matthew 18:15 is so plain, if anyone starts telling you critical or suggestive things about someone else, you know *immediately* they are directly sinning against God. Indeed, if we find ourselves often sitting and speculating about sins in other people's lives, we are already in major sin. No matter who they or how "sweet" and "sincere" their tone of voice, gossipers commit a most serious and damaging sin. In fact, in most cases God considers what they are doing (gossip and slander) far worse than the supposed sin of the person they are discussing! Yet some people have a near-obsessive fascination with hearing and sharing rumors and speculations. They are always hungry for the latest bit of salacious news. Friends, it is absolutely crucial that we come to see gossip and slander for what they are — *vile sins* against God, people and church unity.

We see a further disturbing symptom when people say, "Well, I don't know why, but people are always coming to me to share complaints and gripes." Those individuals often even seem to take pride in the fact people come to them with complaints and concerns. While in one sense it may suggest they have people's confidence, it also suggests something of profound concern. It suggests others know they will listen to their gossip and will *not* follow Matthew 18:15. People are usually "gossip magnets" because others know they will not hold them accountable to obey God's clear command in Scripture. If a believer is committed to follow God's pattern of holiness, it is amazing how quickly gossips stop seeking them out. Yet if we are willing accomplices, they will come to us in droves. In fact, it definitely is *not* a good sign when grumblers and gossips consider us a friendly ear. Make no mistake — willfully receiving ungodly speech is nothing less than serious, direct disobedience to God. (1 Corinthians 5:11; 2 Thessalonians 3:11-14)

Innuendo and Premature Assumptions

We observe an especially damaging pattern in church members who are prone to make snap assumptions and premature judgments about people or situations. These individuals typically form opinions on very little information and make quick assumptions that often prove to be wrong. Yet they voice their opinions "as facts" to virtually anyone who will listen. Untold damage is done when church members judge others without making sure they really know the facts. These patterns are tragically common and become a fertile breeding ground for broken relationships and slanderous gossip. Little more damages churches or hinders God's Spirit than those who draw quick conclusions and then widely voice those thoughts and suspicions.

One of the most devilish forms of gossip and slander is the wicked art of "innuendo." In this form of evil, the perpetrators make statements that simply plant subtle seeds of doubt about someone's character or competence. While they may not come out and make a direct accusation, they are very adept at raising questions that cast suspicion. One of their common ploys is to say "*I heard such and such*" when in fact, the question really came from their own mind. Yet another evil pattern is when they say "*Lots of people are saying*" when in fact, the only comments are from them and one or two others in whom they themselves initiated the questions. When you hear these tell-tale phrases of gossips, huge red flags should immediately raise in your spirit. While such statements do not always represent exaggeration and gossip, many times they are major warning signs.

In actuality, innuendo is often just a sneaky (somewhat cowardly) way of attack and gossip. Under the guise of simply "sharing a concern" or "seeking information," people are actually spreading damaging suspicions and rumors. Of course, there are times when carefully sharing concerns or information is legitimate. But when this becomes a "pattern" and is more about speculative talk than prayer, something is seriously wrong. Satan is indeed a master at planting small doubts then skillfully fanning them into raging fires.

The Tongue — A Raging Fire and World of Evil
(James 3:6-13)

It is truly astounding to see the enormous damage that often comes from simply raising a few suggestive questions. Small suggestions can easily become a sweeping wildfire of gossip and rumor. Sadly enough, some know just where to drop an innuendo to see it quickly explode through the grapevine. In most churches we can hear the same common statement, "If you tell so and so, it's as good as putting it on the six o'clock news." Such statements would be humorous if they were not so tragically true. In many ways, the devil's most reliable and destructive tool is the willing tongue of a gossiper. (James 3:5-6) Godly people should in no way lend an ear to those who consistently exhibit these destructive patterns of sinful speech. Yet today, far too many fail to treat gossip and innuendo with the utter seriousness they deserve.

A related variation of evil speech occurs when people make hurtful or accusatory statements and then say, "Oh, I was only kidding." Some individuals are quite adept at making negative insinuations or verbal jabs under the guise of "making fun." Typically they will also say, "Well I really did not mean anything by it." Just because someone smiles when they malign or criticize makes it no less harmful. In fact, it is an especially devious and subtle form of slander. This form of deceptive malicious speech fools no one and is certainly not funny to God. In Proverbs 26:18, God likens this type of joking to a *"madman throwing burning wood at people."*

Negative Speech — It Is No Laughing Matter!

Shamefully, such unbiblical patterns typically persist in churches because godly members sit back and say little. There is a disturbing tendency for churches to more or less "tolerate" people who spread malicious gossip. Members may try to laugh it off and say, "That's just old so and so, don't pay him (or her) any mind." But the problem is people *do* pay them mind. Make no mistake — negative speech does enormous harm and seriously grieves the Holy Spirit. Worse yet, people who gossip in the church, typically share the same poisons out in the community. Their habits thus do severe damage to the witness and testimony of God's people. Be assured, God finds absolutely nothing humorous or insignificant about gossip and negative speech. He views this sin with extreme seriousness and so too must believers and churches.

Furthermore, this issue cannot be something about which only the pastor is concerned. Until the church body takes it serious and starts biblically dealing with gossip, it will surely continue its deadly cycle. When churches ignore or down-play gossip, these wicked patterns continue year after year! Believers, if we let obvious evil triumph because we're afraid to "cause a controversy," we are ashamed to stand for Christ and His Church. This is often nothing less than a real form of "denying Christ before men."

Diligently Guarding Peace — The Job of Every Church Member
(Ephesians 4:3)

It is *every member's* responsibility to guard the fellowship and unity of a church! If any member hears someone spread gossip, innuendo or unrest, they must lovingly ask them to stop the conversation and immediately follow Matthew 18:15. Be prepared to read the passage and urge their compliance. If they refuse and persist in gossip, you should write down what they are saying, date it and take it straight to key church leadership. When gossipers are quickly held accountable for what they spread, they soon cease the pattern. You may also find they will frequently deny what they said or say that is not what they meant. That is why documentation and witnesses are often important in getting to the truth.

Friend, if you have any degree of spiritual depth, God is counting on you to help deal with such ungodly patterns in your church. A quote from Edmond Burke most clearly captures this important truth. "*The only thing necessary for the triumph of evil is for good men to do nothing.*" Thank God, more and more churches are embracing written covenants to avoid gossip and to squarely address it when it occurs. In light of today's conditions, it is vital that congregations periodically pray through a cleansing resource, to correct any drift toward gossip and disunity. Occasional special emphases can be vital to helping individuals and whole churches renew their covenants to unity.

Yet, as churches or individuals address patterns of gossip, it is always crucial to carefully seek God's wisdom for *when* and *how* to deal with these conditions. It is never wise to confront or make judgments of others rashly. Neither is it advisable to just "up and do something" without much prayer, careful thought and godly council. To act apart from God's method, timing and wisdom could easily create even worse problems. Let us again remember the definitive words of James. *"For man's anger does not bring about the righteous life that God desires."* (James 1:20) There are actually some very simple things believers can do to greatly lessen the incidence of slanderous gossip. Among the most effective is simply turning a deaf ear and denying an audience to gossip and innuendo. To do less is to *aid and abet* the spread of hurtful, negative speech.

Carefully Avoid the "Aiding and Abetting" Syndrome

A common way we inadvertently encourage gossip is by giving a willing ear to one who consistently questions and slanders others. Though they may tell you, "I need to talk," you are not helping by letting them endlessly vent anger or slanderous talk behind someone's back. The truth is, people who tend to gossip often cease their habit if others stop listening! People with this sin pattern typically want an audience quite badly. Yet, when you give them a sympathetic ear, you definitely become an enabler, encourager and accomplice in the sinful pattern.

We must also be aware that people with this habit usually do not see themselves as gossipers. It is amazing how they think what they are doing is somehow "different" and not really gossip. *They may even gossip about how bad old so and so gossips!* People caught in this cycle often have a real blindspot to what they are causing in the lives of others. For this reason, these individuals need your prayers and loving Scripture-based rebuke, and not your tacit participation. In 1 Corinthians 5:11, Paul commanded believers to have nothing to do with a believer who is a "reviler." A reviler is one who is verbally abusive or seriously slanderous toward others. Sadly, we must also note that many do not have a blindspot — they know *exactly* what they are doing!

If you choose to sit and passively listen to a slanderous person, you, in a direct sense, participate in their evil. Without meaning to, you are actually aiding and abetting these damaging sin patterns. The scriptural approach is to lovingly (but firmly) *stop* them and say, "Let's immediately follow Matthew 18:15 and go to the individual you're now taking about." If done in the right spirit, you may help the erring one see their wrong and repent. You may also help them move to a point of reconciliation and healing. Yet unfortunately, in many cases people ensnared in this pattern have little desire to actually take the biblical steps. Sadly, they usually just want to talk behind the person's back. If you suggest the biblical course of reconciliation and they refuse or change the subject, you must generally conclude this person is not interested in truly obeying God.

While slanderous gossip is tragically common, it is only one of many forms of evil now sweeping countless churches. To our shame, we live in a day when attacks on pastors, staff, lay-leaders and church fellowship are taking ever more varied and vicious forms. Concerning this point, we must all remember one vital truth. *When we attack fellow believers, we are directly attacking the unity and love of Christ's Church.* Scriptures leave no doubt that to attack the unity of Christ's Church is to attack Christ! Dear reader, if God is speaking to the depths of you heart, I am confident you now sense His voice. Please do not become defensive or resist His Word. He always receives the broken and contrite but always resists the proud. (Psalm 101:5) Reflect on His voice through these closing words.

Grace to Claim
(1 John 1:9)

As you read this section, did God bring specific patterns to your mind that you need to confess and forsake? Please take a moment and look back through the different headings in this section. What very specific things do you need to confess? Be very specific and thorough. I will even suggest that you write them down. Above all, rest in the confidence that Jesus' blood is greater than your greatest sins! "*Therefore there is now no condemnation for those who are in Christ Jesus.*" (Romans 8:1)

Steps to Take
(Proverbs 28:13)

First, it is vital to understand that confession alone is not repentance. In fact, confession doesn't become complete without the elements of repentance, restitution and reconciliation. *"He who conceals his sins does not prosper: but whoever **confesses** and **forsakes** them finds mercy."* (Proverbs 28:13) *"Therefore if you are offering your gift at the altar and there remember that your brother has something against you, leave your gift there in front of the altar. First go and be reconciled to your brother; then come and offer your gift."* (Matthew 5:23-24) *"For if you forgive men when they sin against you, your heavenly Father will also forgive you: But if you do not forgive men their sins, your Father will not forgive your sins."* (Matthew 6:14-15) My friend, God will surely give you grace to make your necessary steps of change.

Second, God will lead us to ask forgiveness of particular people we have in some way hurt or offended (either directly or indirectly). An excellent way to know if you need to go to someone is by considering the following question: When you and others read some of these sections, do you believe you come to the minds of certain people when they read the same sections? If your honest answer is yes, it is very possible you now have your answer for steps of reconciliation that are needed. If fellow church or family members think of you when they read these sections, you can know there is a need for change.

Ask God for wisdom and get spiritual council as you prepare to seek forgiveness and reconciliation from others. If you carefully follow God's leading, you will be amazed at the incredible sense of peace in following His guidance. Above all, remember His wonderful grace and acceptance even now. He is with you from the first moment you resolve to seek and do His will! Since this is a pilot book, I will not include "Grace to Claim & Steps to Take" after each of the twenty-four revival hindrances. Simply follow these simple sections with each Pattern and God will revolutionize your life. Obey His voice and rest in His glorious love and grace!

Words of Hope and Life

Proverbs 28:13 – *"He that covers his sins shall not prosper: but whoso confesses and forsakes them shall have mercy."*

Isaiah 1:18 - *"Come now and let us reason together, says the Lord; though your sins be as scarlet, they shall be as white as snow; though they be red like crimson, they shall be as wool."*

Joel 2:12-13 (KJV) – *"Therefore also now, saith the Lord, Turn ye even to Me with all your heart, and with fasting, and with weeping, and with mourning: And rend your heart, and not your garments, and turn unto the Lord your God: for He is gracious and merciful, slow to anger, and of great kindness, and repenteth him of the evil."*

I John 1:9 – *"If we confess our sins, He is faithful and just to forgive us our sins, and to cleanse us from all unrighteousness."*

Pattern Three
Revolving-Door Pastors and
Disappearing Members

(Psalm 105:15; 1 Corinthians 1:10;
1 Thessalonians 5:12-13; 1 Timothy 5:17)

In some churches, there is a disturbing repeating pattern of getting rid of preachers or staff after only a short tenure. Make no mistake — a long history of mistreating leaders is strong indication of profound spiritual problems. Indeed, little could be more unscriptural or detrimental to kingdom work. Little could bring greater shame to the name of Christ and His Church. Not only does this devastate people in the church, it presents a horrible witness to the unchurched community. Jesus said the world would know we are His by our love; instead, they are wholly repulsed by our anger and division. (John 13:34-35) When we cannot treat God's servants with civility, it rightly makes us an object of derision and scorn to the lost world.

*Author's note: Fellow believers, I deeply wish this was not a section I was required to write. I assure you it is written with many tears and prayerful deliberation. As I researched this matter, I have felt something of the broken heart of God over this issue. While every revival hindrance is serious, little more grieves God's heart than bitter battles between church members and their pastors or leaders. *Yet in recent years, there has been a shocking explosion of mistreating Christian leaders over smaller and often subjective issues.* One thing is certain — revival will surely tarry until these patterns are addressed and reconciliation fully sought for past offenses. However, I have great news for even the most discouraged church or

reader. God is at work and some pastors and churches *are* finding reconciliation! Best of all, some are finding glorious victory by seeking forgiveness and healing for past battles. *No one can fully move forward until they have settled the past.* Yet, to God's praise, even the most seemingly hopeless people and churches can find incredible transformation.

However for balance, I also state we are seeing far too many instances where pastors or leaders committed major offenses that their churches were forced to address. The conditions we cover in the coming paragraphs, do not include those situations in which pastors or leaders were in such error that their churches had to act. Laypersons in such situations have God's deepest compassion and support. In fact, over years of conferences, I have known many godly laypersons whom God mightily used to get churches through stormy waters and unavoidable leadership changes. But in every case they carefully followed biblical principles, moved with loving caution, and often sought wise counsel from denominational leaders. These dear lay-leaders are to be much admired and the patterns addressed in the following section in no way refer to them. Thank God, His grace is truly sufficient for whatever conditions we face. Best of all, there is glorious hope for every person and church. But now we must turn our attention to the dangerous revival hindrance of the mistreatment of God's leaders by their churches.

Before examining these specific hindrances, we should note that some have certainly become involved in wrong patterns with no real intent of doing harm. In some cases, people have never been taught the biblical patterns of leading ministers to and from churches. Sometimes those who end up harming churches and ministers actually had good intentions at the outset. Satan is indeed a master at deceiving us into doing his bidding. This section is designed to unmask fleshly patterns that are definitely not from God.

Remember dear reader, if God opens your eyes to formally unrealized areas of sin, He is doing it to lift you up, not hurt you. He knows you were really trying to do the right thing. Humbly and honestly confess whatever wrong He reveals and you will find glorious grace and restoration. However, several patterns described in this section are so obviously evil, *no one* could do them innocently. It is especially urgent that you immediately confess and forsake any such patterns.

A Tragic Repeating Pattern

As we study nationwide trends of mistreating leaders, distinct patterns become evident. Surveys show unscriptural patterns usually revolve around a relatively small power group who take it upon themselves to decide when preachers come and go. Unfortunately, this most damaging behavior follows an all-too predictable pattern. Based on extensive study and conference experience, I must report the following scenario is almost as predictable as clockwork. Relatively soon after the pastor's arrival, there will be some area of disagreement or supposed shortcoming. (Of course, sooner or later we all disagree on something.) But rather than lovingly working through areas of disagreement, the power group quickly comes to their usual solution — "Let's just get rid of him!"

They next enter a period of finding many faults with the minister and soon initiate a phone and gossip campaign to drain away his support. To those individuals, the leader just cannot seem to do anything right and they promote that view to all who will listen. They relentlessly look for ways to *magnify* his faults (which every minister and church member certainly has) and *minimize* his positives. Though it sounds unbelievable, it is not at all uncommon for some people to literally trump up false accusations or start rumors. Once they have decided they do not like a pastor, staff person or lay-leader, they adopt what could only be called a "scorched earth" policy. To get their way, they are often willing to seriously damage or destroy the reputations of virtually anyone and everyone in their path.

According to Scripture, such profound wickedness puts people at escalated risk of God's correction. We should also understand that at least the *principle* of "touching not God's anointed" can apply not only to attacking pastors and staff, but also laypersons who are being much used of the Lord. Yet, rather than developing the spiritual maturity to biblically work through areas of conflict, the godless approach is to quickly dump fellow believers or abruptly cut-off relationships so we can supposedly move on and "start all over." Little could be more unbiblical or opposite to the ways of God! After all, Jesus said our primary witness to the lost world is to be our incredible love and unity. (John 13:34-35;17:21) Such attitudes and behaviors break God's heart and devastate His work in a church.

"It's Just Time for a Change"

A related form of this condition occurs when a minister has been with a church for some years and a small power group decides "It's just time for a change." Under that little phrase a literal world of ungodly behavior is committed against pastors, staff and lay-leaders. And even though grievances against a pastor are often relatively minor and subjective, God's servant is essentially handed his walking papers. Though he may have faithfully led and suffered with the people through many valleys, all of that is easily forgotten. After all, in the minds of such individuals, the minister is just an "expendable hired hand we can fire at will." Very little could be more unbiblical or less like the attitude of Christ. God will not indefinitely tolerate such carnal, unscriptural patterns for treating His servants or conducting church. Sooner or later, God's chastisement comes to churches or individuals who persistently practice such godless patterns. His holiness and concern for kingdom work cannot allow such conditions to continue indefinitely.

Of course, the above patterns are the direct opposite of God's way for leading ministers to and from churches. They are also opposite of anything even remotely resembling loving or mature Christian behavior. If believers stubbornly persist in the more extreme forms of these sinful patterns, they run serious risk of God's intervention, especially after God convicts them. Yet because of deep spiritual blindness, it never crosses their minds that God may deal severely with those who persist in causing such major problems in churches. (1 Corinthians 11:30; Acts 5:1-11)

God's Toleration is not Endless

It would likely shock us to realize the times God had to deal strongly with people for seriously hindering His work in a church. While it certainly grieves Him to intervene, His holiness and concern for Christ's Church often requires an eventual response. After years of nationwide research, I could publish a massive book comprised solely of sobering reports where God apparently intervened to stop persons damaging the unity in His Church. Of course, I would never publish such a book because only God knows for certain which events are judgment and which are not. But one thing is certain — the Bible leaves *no doubt* that God will not indefinitely tolerate such damaging, ungodly behavior in a local congregation. (Acts 5:1-11; 1 Corinthians 11:28-34; Hebrews 10:26,31)

People must never think that the fact they seem to have gotten away with it, is any sign that they will continue to go un-judged. God's judgment may grind slowly but it grinds *surely*. (Galatians 6:7; 1 Peter 4:17) Furthermore when God brings clear attention to a particular sin, His potential judgment just drew much closer. (Luke 12:48) Once we fully recognize something as sin and *then* stubbornly resist obedience, consequences are much more certain and serious!

Dear readers, it is profoundly dangerous to make excuses or try and explain away God's clear conviction. If He has revealed areas of sin, please do not resist or be angered by His reproof. Humble yourself and you will be blessed beyond measure! Remember — God *never* rejects the broken and contrite but *always* resists the proud. (Psalm 51:17; James 4:6) I am forced to stress this issue for one vital reason. There are growing indications that God is about to send a revival and contrary to popular understanding, revivals often begin with increased judgment! (1 Peter 4:17)

A related symptom of a spiritually troubled church is rapid turnover of members. Where unloving attitudes are present, people that do join the church often quickly stop attending or move their membership. When people sense love and unity in a church, they want to establish relationships and get involved. However, if they don't sense love and warmth, they either drop out of regular attendance or quickly leave the church. If a church has a lot of "fruit basket turnover," it is very important to ask why. While high turnover is not always the fault of a church, it usually suggests a major problem of fellowship.

Dear reader, has God convicted you of any of the patterns described in this section? If so, please do not become defensive or argue with God. We never win and always lose when we resist the clear teaching of God's Word. Again, please remember God's reason for conviction: He seeks only to bring repentance and transformation into your life. If you heed His voice, miraculous change and growth will surely occur. When you go to anyone you may have wronged, healing will flow like a river. Let us seek Him while He may yet be found. (Isaiah 55:6)

Pattern Four
The "They're not Our Kind" Syndrome

(Matthew 28:16-18; James 2:1-4: 1 John 4:7-8)

An especially shocking revival barrier is when some members actually attack pastors or staff who are leading a church to significant evangelism and growth. It is utterly astounding that some long-standing members attack church growth by statements such as, "they're just not our kind." It is truly shocking that any believer would actually say such a thing. Since Jesus said our whole purpose is to reach *all* people, this attitude is nothing less than an *abomination*! According to James 2:1-5, it is difficult to imagine how any saved person could do anything but rejoice when people are being reached (regardless of their "kind"). Such attitudes represent profound immaturity, spiritual blindness or worse.

Just about the most spiritually dangerous thing anyone can do is attack or hinder someone who is reaching souls for Christ. When someone is attacking evangelism or missions, there can be little doubt who is the real author of that attack. It certainly isn't the Holy Spirit! Mark this well — God will have little or nothing to do with any church (or person) that draws a line and only wants to minister to "certain people." Even the slightest hint of such an attitude is against all that Christ represents! *No one* who walks with God could ever show such blatant partiality or prejudice. (James 2:1-9) These attitudes are the very opposite of Christ's heart of love for all people!

Still others harshly attack successful leaders because, in their words, "*things are changing in our church.*" While it is certainly true that not all change is good, reaching large numbers of new people always means some level of change. The fact is, we cannot stay frozen in time and growth will bring some differences. Yet some people are so self-focused and set in their ways, they demand everything to stay just like they want it. To them, the desires, needs and tastes of others simply do not matter. Even if they see the church reaching far more people by making some changes, they really don't care. People with this problem often become very vicious in their attitudes toward those leaders who "brought the changes."

Yet another reason some attack a successful leader is when a power group fears a "loss of control." Many churches are plagued by those who really do not want pastors or staff to be "too successful" because it may lessen their (power group's) influence. Such reasoning is in no way biblical or Spirit-guided! Sadly enough, when a power group fears a pastor or leader is becoming "too popular" they often start magnifying his faults or exaggerating problems to make them seem worse. They hardly notice good points and dwell continually on real or imagined faults. In many cases, we even hear of people finding subtle ways to sabotage people's ministries and relationships. All the while, these attitudes and behaviors devastate the activity of God in their congregation.

Some people are so utterly godless and jealous of power, they are not above *inventing* scandal or crises to try and drive off a leader. It is doubtful that any truly saved person would ever commit such blatant evil. If a Christian ever did sink to such wickedness, the Bible clearly teaches that he or she should *expect* strong chastisement from God. Anyone involved in such patterns should take Psalm 105:15 very seriously (especially if God is now clearly speaking to your heart). "*Do not touch my anointed ones.*" According to Hebrews, continuing in willful sin after knowing better is to *stomp* on the precious blood of Jesus.

Questions for Reflection

Is there any sense in which you have exhibited prejudice toward certain persons or groups? Have you drawn distinctions and sought only to reach people you consider more desirable? God's Word leaves no doubt as to His attitude toward selective ministry. It is a behavior that draws His severest displeasure and reprimand.

Have you in any way attacked or criticized church leaders for reaching certain people or leading your church to growth? While it is certainly true that change and growth are challenging, this gives no one the right to become bitter or unkind toward others.

Dear saint, if God has convicted you in any of these areas, He is pointing you to forgiveness, healing and transformation. Confess any sin and trust Him for grace to change. Instead of a hindrance, you will become a powerful catalyst for revival!

Pattern Five
Attack and Resistance Toward
the "New People"

(John 17:20-22; Acts 2:1,42-47; Romans 15:5-7)

Another form of attack is when long-term members express hostility or resistance toward newer people who take positions of leadership. In some churches, long-standing members seek to maintain "control" at all costs. This can be an especially serious problem in smaller churches when one or two families may seek to control everything tightly. Mature believers rejoice when God grows their church and are thrilled for others to share leadership. Yet pastors and other leaders are often angrily attacked simply for seeking to involve a broader group in leadership. Little could be more selfish, prideful or ungodly. But for just such reasons, godly leaders are increasingly under fire.

Churches with this pattern tend to have a distinct attitude of cliquishness among longer term members. Rather than following God's command to function as a loving family and unified body, it tends to be difficult for new members to fully feel a part. While admittedly assimilating new members takes real effort and loving patience, it is among the most central elements of our calling as Christ's Church. In fact, we are to be totally committed to doing whatever it takes to welcome and involve new members, not make them feel marginalized. Little worse could be said of a church than the label of being unloving or cold to visitors and new members. *After all, the very heart of God's purpose is that we be a loving body, functioning as one.* (John 13:34-35; 17:20-22)

Whether or not they realize it, people are badly hindering God's Spirit when they resist involving new members in the heart of church life. A church is to function as a body with many people using their gifts in service. It is not to be a monopoly with only a few people doing everything. However, in churches where no one will step up to the plate of service, a few people may indeed have to do it all. In such cases these people are to be admired, not criticized. People who will not work have no right to criticize those who at least get up and try. Yet it is amazing how some people will sit on the sidelines and continually criticize those who are actually doing the heavy lifting. These individuals are typically full of advice and instructions until the question turns to their possibly shouldering a major work load themselves.

Dear believer, have you resisted God's command to welcome and embrace new members in your church? Without question, we are to work to assimilate new members in the ministry of Christ's Church. Have you in any way been jealous or possessive of power? Do you at all exhibit a "we/they" attitude in the body of Christ? Cliques and factions should have no place in the Church. In fact, this was the exact attitude that caused God to severely judge several members of the Corinthian church. (1 Corinthians 11:28-34) May God grant us the wisdom to live and love as one family.

Pattern Six
Worship Wars and Generational Battles

(Romans 12:9(a),16-18; 1 Corinthians 3:1-3;12:25-27)

A most serious hindrance is the tendency for some to attack others angrily when the music style is not always what ministers to them. Church leadership has the difficult task of seeking ways to lead the widest range of people into genuine worship. It shows gross selfishness and immaturity when someone cares only about "their own tastes" and has little or no concern for the needs of others. For believers, the central issue should always be what is best for the kingdom and the widest range of people. Yet for the carnal and immature, the central issue is, "How can I have everything exactly like I want it."

While attacks on worship style are often couched in spiritual or doctrinal objections, the real issues are usually personal taste and plain selfishness. (Though there are exceptions when objections are indeed doctrinal and legitimate.) It is my conviction that far extremes on either end of the scale should generally be avoided. If each group shows love and basic maturity, we can almost always meet peacefully somewhere in the middle. Yet, if each group is determined to have it all "their way," the fight is on! Of all things, there is something profoundly sad about believers fighting over worship.

Generational battles usually occur when young and old view one another with a general attitude of criticism and suspicion. While some natural generational tensions are to be expected, it can easily move into sinful attitudes of disrespect (both ways). We must all remember that different generations have had very varied experiences, so some of their tastes and views will naturally be different. Yet rather than seeking to understand and accept some of these differences, each group writes off the other as "unspiritual" or "out of touch." Battles lines are drawn and each group becomes antagonistic and withdraws from the other.

Bitter generational battles are completely opposite from the principle of unity in diversity as described in Scripture. (1 Corinthians 12-14) It is healthy for diverse age groups and cultures to work through the process of developing the maturity to abide together in peace. Spiritual maturity definitely requires "give and take" from each group. Yet today, many want to selfishly draw a circle and only be around those just like themselves. This is clearly *not* the New Testament pattern and actually robs us of an essential element of spiritual growth.

Different Generations Truly Need One Another!

Serious age-related battles are especially sad because each group actually has so much to give to the other. The truth is, we really do need each other! Today's young desperately need the loving encouragement and guidance of senior adults, *not* their harsh condemnation. On the other hand, seniors deserve the honor, respect and ministry of younger generations. Clearly, God calls both groups to work at being loving and understanding toward the other. It is a great tragedy to see issues like music or cultural styles bring anger, suspicion and unnecessary separation.

An increasingly common failure is when seniors harshly over-criticize children and youth who are somewhat unruly in church. It is vital to remember many of these children come from chaotic schools and dysfunctional families with no church background whatsoever. How could we possibly expect them to automatically know how to act in church? While we certainly cannot give up on maintaining reasonable order, we must show love and patience toward today's youth. The last thing they need is to attend church and experience anger, harshness and condemnation from older believers. If their first brief encounters in church are decidedly negative, they will likely reject Christ and never return to *any* church. Dear saints, our attitudes may be the first (and potentially last) impression many ever receive of the Savior.

Reaching today's unchurched generation is indeed a challenging venture. They often come to our churches with no biblical knowledge, wounded lives and deep bondages. If we draw self-righteous robes around ourselves and mostly meet them with harsh condemnation, we could not be acting less like Christ. While we certainly cannot compromise biblical standards and truth, we must show love and understanding in guiding younger generations toward spiritual growth. It is essential that older believers show the maturity and patience to love generations whose cultures differ vastly from their own. Let us ever remember that "love covers a multitude of sins" and crosses an ocean of barriers. (1 Peter 4:8) In other words, love sees past earrings, purple hair and tattoos!

At the same time, it is equally vital for churches to teach children and youth to honor and respect senior adults. Youth leaders must work hard at helping youth appreciate the strengths and wisdom of older generations. After all, honoring seniors is a biblical command! The younger generation should be taught to consider the feelings of seniors, not willfully flaunt offensive behaviors in their faces. Rather than ignoring their feelings, younger generations should avoid disrespect and insensitivity toward their elders. Though cultures, music and tastes are starkly different, young and old must both work at showing loving consideration for the other. Christ's love and unity demands that different generations work at meeting somewhere in the middle. *"Each of you should look not only to your own interests, but also to the interests of others."* (Philippians 2:4)

We are seldom more like Christ than when we move past our comfort zones to love those who are different. Conversely, we are seldom more like the devil than when we selfishly demand our way or disregard the needs of others. It is wonderful to note that some groups of senior adults and youth are working to love one another in spite of differences. Is this happening in your church or are battle lines still drawn? My friend, why wait on others to make the first move? God may well be calling you to deny yourself and take steps to make peace for the good of Christ's Church. One thing is certain — no believer can afford to shut off dialogue with other parts of the body of Christ. When we follow that path we all lose and Christ's name is shamed.

Pattern Seven
Clock Watching, Fleshly Complaining and Spiritual Insensitivity

The Sin of Insulting the Holy Spirit!
(John 4:23-24; Ephesians 4:30;
1 Thessalonians 5:19-20)

A disturbing modern evil is angry grumbling against leadership when worship services run a few minutes beyond the normal time. Imagine the utter absurdity of telling the Holy Spirit, "You must enter and exit precisely on our time table." One thing is certain — no great move of God has *ever* come with people closely watching a clock. Yet it is clear some have the attitude we're really doing God a favor by giving Him an hour on Sunday. God forbid that we should actually be made to sit for an extra few minutes of hearing His Word. And Lord help the person who would dare make us ten minutes late for lunch!

When individuals gripe and complain over such matters, they reveal a truly shocking level of carnality. The implications of such attitudes are deeply disturbing. Indeed, what does it say about a person's spirituality (or total lack thereof) when they find it difficult to "endure" even a few extra moments of Scripture and worship? How would they be able to tolerate the continuous praise of Heaven? Without question, they would be extremely out of place in the atmosphere of Heaven. Such an astoundingly shallow attitude suggests serious concern for someone's spiritual condition.

Recapturing Reverence for the Preached Word

Another pattern of this sin is great insensitivity to the Holy Spirit *during* worship services. Especially as we move toward decision time, some people begin to shift around, look at their watches or even get up and leave. Anyone remotely sensitive to God knows the invitation (decision time) is absolutely crucial. Especially during that time, the only proper response is to remain quiet, earnestly praying for yourself and those who may need to make decisions. Any other response becomes a tool Satan uses to distract others and grieve the Holy Spirit.

Little is more distracting or hindering to God's Spirit than people shuffling around or leaving while a minister is trying to lead souls to a life or death choice. What does it say about someone if all he or she can think of is "getting out" while people are being asked to make eternal decisions? It can only say they are completely and totally out of touch with God's Spirit! If people are that concerned with getting to lunch or beating others to the parking lot, something is tragically wrong in their souls.

For balance and grace, let me note that some believers may have committed these patterns without realizing how seriously they hinder the Holy Spirit. My friend, if that is your case, God is gracious and knows you did not intend to hinder His Spirit. Simply confess this wrong and resolve to be more sensitive in the future. On the other hand, there are some who know these patterns hinder God's Spirit and really don't care. There is grave concern for anyone with such callous indifference to God and people.

Rejecting the "Worship Spectator" Attitude

A hindrance often overlooked is when believers are mentally and spiritually disengaged while the Word is preached and people are making decisions. God definitely intends for all believers to be spiritual *participants* and not just passive *spectators* in a worship service. When we are present in worship, God expects us to *participate* by actively responding to His Word and praying for others as it is preached. To do less, is to hinder the moving of God's Spirit. Yet, many believers seem unaware they hinder God's Spirit by daydreaming instead of personally responding or praying for others. While this hindrance is certainly not as direct and overt as moving around or leaving early, it is nonetheless significant.

In conclusion, I must also stress the enormous importance of believers immediately obeying whatever prompting God gives in a worship service. Studies show most modern believers have settled into a passive, non-response pattern in worship services. Yet, if we are truly listening and sensitive, God will often prompt us to go to the altar to pray, go to someone needing prayer, commit to some area of repentance or share a testimony or prayer burden. When a church body settles into a continual pattern of doing nothing in response to God's Word, the Holy Spirit is seriously quenched. The moment God speaks, believers must be sensitive to act in obedience. To ignore that prompting badly quenches God's Spirit in the atmosphere of the church.

Preachers and evangelists go into some churches and immediately sense that all too familiar oppressive "wall of resistance." Experienced conference leaders and revivalists often dub this phenomena "the invisible wall." On the other hand, when church members are sensitive and quickly responsive, it is far easier for others to make much needed public decisions. This creates a spiritual freedom in the very atmosphere. In such churches, there is a far greater sense of God's presence and wonderful freedom for people to respond. It is amazing how one person's obedience frees obedience in many others. Sadly, it is also true that one person's disobedience can hinder and quench God's Spirit in a whole congregation. May God help us return to proper sensitivity to His holy presence.

Without question, corporate worship and prayer services are the most crucial times of kingdom activity. If we are to see revival, believers must return to the reverential awe of God's holy presence. In fact, we are commanded to literally *tremble* before His Word. (Isaiah 66:5) If we embrace such an attitude of reverence, all fleshly complaining, careless distractions and cold insensitivity will immediately cease in our services! May God help us return to instant obedience to His smallest prompting. As King of Kings and Lord of Lords, He surely deserves our full attention, absolute reverence and quick obedience.

Dear reader, has God convicted you of any tendency to daydream or neglect prayer during worship services? Have you hindered God's Spirit by moving around or distracting others? Are there times you resist God's clear prompting to go to the altar or pray with your pastor? If you resolve to revere His Word now and promptly respond to His Spirit, neither you nor your church will ever be the same!

Pattern Eight
Prayer Meeting Boycotts
and Fleshly Resistance

(Matthew 21:13; Mark 11:17; Acts 2:1;4:31)

One of the most tragic hindrances sometimes occurs when a church chooses to embrace a genuine weekly prayer meeting. It is sad but true that most "church prayer meetings" have long ago ceased to be actual prayer meetings. Generally, they became Bible studies with a brief "hospital list" prayer at the end. Virtually no prayer is given to the eternal issues of evangelism, missions or revival. Yet to God's praise, a glorious return to prayer meetings is underway! But unbelievably, some church members strongly attack and resist Christ's foremost command for churches to be "houses of prayer." (Matthew 21:13; Mark 11:17) Frankly, it is astounding that any believer would actually attack and complain about the church establishing a weekly meeting that is focused on prayer. To resist the strengthening of prayer meetings is to attack the very heart and purpose of God! But nonetheless, such fleshly resistance is disturbingly common.

Many may object to a weekly churchwide prayer meeting with statements such as the following. "I want Bible study so I can grow — we can pray at home. Our preacher's job is to preach and teach, we can all pray on our own. We pay our preacher to preach, not pray. There is no need for a whole service to pray, we can just say a prayer at the end. I am not good at praying aloud so I will just stop attending if all we're going to do is pray." (Yet no one is required to pray aloud and praying is how we learn to pray better.) While some of these objections may be honest and sincere, they are utterly contrary to Scripture and the practice of the New Testament Church! They are also completely out of touch with The Spirit of God. Such sentiments are the very opposite of any generation that ever saw a great spiritual awakening.

Church Prayer Meetings — A New Testament Requirement!

Without question, *every* church should embrace a strong pattern of powerful churchwide prayer meetings! Both the Old and New Testaments leave no doubt that strong corporate praying is essential to being the people of God. Jesus made this utterly clear with His powerful statement in Matthew 21:13(KJV): *"My house shall be called a house of prayer."* There is no question that the whole practice and power of the New Testament Church centered around corporate prayer. (Acts 1:4;2:1;4:31;6:4,12) Furthermore, every great awakening centered around corporate prayer, biblical preaching and deep repentance.

It is vital to understand that a New Testament church is not defined by doctrine alone! It is defined by doctrine and *practice*. Indeed, how could any church honestly call itself a "New Testament church" if serious corporate prayer meetings are not a predominant practice? After all, was not corporate prayer a central preeminent practice of New Testament Churches? Indeed it was! According to the book of Acts, early churches spent so much time in corporate prayer you could almost say they *were* a prayer meeting! Given these undeniable truths, is it not astounding that so many modern churches decided they could no longer devote even one weekly service to prayer? Friends, it is not only astounding, it is the primary cause of declining conversions, rising disunity and collapsing morals!

Very little could be more unbiblical than to assume we can do fine without churchwide prayer meetings. In light of today's devastating trends, do we really think our activities and outreach strategies can replace prayer meetings? Sadly many apparently still do believe our church programs, activities and preaching can replace humbling ourselves in fervent, united prayer. One thing is certain — God has *never* sent sweeping revival to any generation that arrogantly thought itself "beyond" the need for fervent corporate prayer.

Until we return to this fundamental principle of corporate prayer, we will continue to lack full New Testament power. Yet at long last, there are growing signs of hope. Concerning prayer meetings, there is a cloud the size of a man's hand on the horizon!

A Coming Wave of Prayer Meetings!

God is at work and hundreds of churches are returning to weekly corporate prayer, solemn assemblies, and deeper repentance! After fifty years of near total silence, some seminaries are showing signs of increasing emphasis on these crucial practices. I believe today's increasing prayer meetings and solemn assemblies represent the single greatest sign of a potential coming revival. Yet unbelievably, some church members actually attack and criticize pastors for doing the one thing that can bring revival — church prayer meetings! It speaks volumes about the negative spiritual level of anyone who would resist prayer meetings or boycott these services. After all, prayer meetings are the very *heart* of Christians' spiritual power and fellowship.

For sake of balance and fairness, let me state that some prayer meeting resistance comes out of honest misunderstanding or fear. Since most have never been taught these truths, many truly do not understand *why* church prayer meetings are so important. Still others are insecure and intimidated by a prayer meeting simply because they've never been *taught* to pray effectively. As leaders, we cannot expect our people to automatically understand the significance of prayer meetings if we haven't clearly taught them! Indeed, how could we expect them to be comfortable or proficient at praying together if we have not modeled it or instructed them? While attacking or boycotting prayer meetings is a truly egregious sin, pastors must show patience in lovingly leading our people toward deeper prayer and understanding.

As a practical help, pastors are encouraged to have their entire congregation to read the book, *Biblical Patterns for Powerful Church Prayer Meetings*. This inexpensive book is designed to fully convince believers of the importance and practicality of conducting powerful prayer meetings. A related book is entitled *Seeking the Reviver—Not Just Revival, Personal and Corporate Prayers that Please God and Bring Awakening*. A third book, *How to Develop an Evangelistic Kingdom-focused Church Prayer Ministry* also addresses the subject of corporate prayer and cleansing. All three books can be secured from the Oklahoma Baptist General Convention for very nominal costs! Once church members truly understand the biblical necessity and awesome benefits of corporate prayer meetings, they will be far more than ready to embrace them. To the praise of God, thousands of churches are beginning to do just that!

Pattern Nine
Business Meeting Ambushes and
"Get Out the Vote" Power Plays

(Proverbs 6:16(d); Matthew 5:9;
1 Thessalonians 5:13b-15)

An especially damaging form of spiritual attack is when church members wait for a public meeting to "spring" some issue or grievance on their leadership in a churchwide setting. I call this pattern "the business meeting ambush." Not only does this totally violate Matthew 18:15, it is usually a sneaky attempt to force an agenda or to attack, belittle and embarrass church leaders. After all, we are commanded to deal with issues privately if at all possible. Yet instead of going to church leaders and discussing or informing them of a matter beforehand, some individuals purposely wait in order to make a public scene. This is unbiblical and contrary to the Spirit of Christ.

Closely related is the very ungodly behavior of the phone campaign to get inactive members to come to that one meeting and back a particular position. It is hard to imagine how non-attendees would have the gall to show up and then of course promptly disappear again. To assure they "get their way," words and motions are carefully preplanned down to who will quickly jump up, second the motion and call for the vote.

Some actually plan devious ways to keep potential opposition from being in the meeting. They may even orchestrate a "surprise" business meeting when key opposing leaders are out of town. People who commit such deceits are often so utterly out of touch with God, they will even brag about these tactics and congratulate themselves for what they think is clever maneuvering. It is difficult to imagine how any Christian could think such behavior is the way to conduct God's business. Yet today, such fleshly machinations are all too common.

Of course, these fleshly behaviors often lead to angry, bitter battles in business meetings. If battles do not erupt in the actual meeting, these patterns surely lead to serious anger and divisiveness under the surface. Worse yet, such practices profoundly quench and grieve the Holy Spirit. (Ephesians 4:30) Business meetings and decisions of these types often set back churches' ministries for months or even years. Such behavior greatly damages our ability to evangelize and is an absolute disgrace to the name of Christ. (John 13:34-35;17:21) God is deeply offended and angered by such godlessness committed in His name. In Scripture, it is very clear that Holy God cannot tolerate such flesh-guided patterns in His Church forever.

Though this subject is painful, God assures readers of mercy if we genuinely repent. Indeed, there may be several reading this section who have never been taught the error of some of the behaviors we have chronicled. It is entirely possible you have seen church business conducted in these ways from your earliest memory. God is especially merciful to those who sinned unintentionally. My friend, God is ready to forgive, heal and restore! Whatever you do, please do not make excuses, resist or become angry at His reproof. If God has opened your eyes to sin, He has done it for one reason — to forgive you and change your life! But also be aware, when He clearly speaks, our accountability to obey rises many fold. The choice is yours — revival or rebellion. Oh dear reader, please let it be revival and blessing.

Pattern Ten
Victory Over Pot Stirring
and Ax Grinding

(Ephesians 4:29-32; Philippians 4:8; James 5:9)

Still another expression of ungodliness occurs when some people keep "stirring the pot" of controversy even after the church has clearly expressed its will on a matter. Unless an issue is truly over some fundamental doctrine, believers must have the maturity and good judgment to live in peace though the church decision may not best suit them. After all, the majority could be right and we should have the humility to submit to the greater good. While it takes genuine humility and maturity to embrace this pattern, it is certainly God's will that we do so.

If a church member's disagreement is truly over fundamental doctrine, he or she should probably pray about going to a church that agrees with their conviction (rather than staying and angrily disrupting fellowship). Yet in far too many cases, individuals just keep grinding the axe of controversy. Worse yet, they often do everything possible to make the church decision fail. Sadly, we see this when those who didn't vote to call a particular pastor actually work directly or indirectly to undermine his ministry. They will tend to minimize his positives and maximize any weaknesses. Very little could be more immature or damaging to God's work.

Another form of this evil is seen in those who consistently seek to stir up controversies where none even exist. Some people have gotten trapped in such negative mindsets they just aren't content unless they are complaining or pointing out some "problem." These individuals have very little positive to say no matter how well things may be going in most areas. People with this pattern are almost always complaining or unhappy about something. Not only is this extremely damaging to the spirit of a church, it is serious sin and direct disobedience to God.

In Philippians 4:8, we are clearly commanded to keep our focus on things that are good and positive. *"Finally, brothers, whatever is noble, whatever is right, whatever is pure, whatever is lovely, whatever is admirable — if anything is excellent or praiseworthy — think about such things."* (Philippians 4:8) In other words, we are only to glance at one another's weaknesses (which we all have) and gaze at the positives. Thank God, we really can learn to be positive and up-building to others. Furthermore, when negative people become more positive, the entire church is blessed and so are they. By God's grace, even the most complaining heart can become faith-filled, positive and encouraging to others.

"Across the Aisle" Revivals

The turning point in most great revivals is not when people go "down" the aisle but "across the aisle" to get right with others. When angry, divided believers take the first steps and go to one another, God often sends a flood of His Spirit! Dear believer, God is waiting on you to turn from your anger, criticism, and judgment. When you take the first step toward getting right with God and others, He will take ten toward you!

Pattern Eleven
Robbing God to Protest People

(Malachi 3:8-10; Luke 6:38; Galatians 6:7-9)

A serious form of hindrance is when some members withhold tithes because of a particular church decision or circumstance. In essence, this is blatant disobedience to the God who commands us to bring all the tithes into the storehouse. Furthermore, He did not command the tithe *unless* you don't happen to like some church decision. Failure to tithe is plain robbery and a direct affront to God. (Malachi 3:8-10) Just because we disagree with a particular decision, we have no right to rob God. If a situation is truly that serious, then parties should go find a church they can support. On the other hand, if it really isn't a vital issue and they leave simply because they're angry, God's Spirit is seriously grieved in their lives. No matter where they may go, they go without the blessing and favor of God.

For the most part, withholding the tithe is a sinful way some try to punish others for not doing things their way. The tithe should be viewed as holy and not a tool for opposing people or policies we do not like. Robbing God is no way to protest our disagreement with the decisions or shortcomings of people! In fact, God warns of severe consequences to those who rob Him *regardless* of the reason. (Malachi 3:9) Dear saints, we must return to the understanding that the tithe is a most holy part of our worship to God, not some bargaining chip to punish people. Neither is God's tithe a device for threatening others to get our way. It is profoundly dangerous to play fleshly games with God's holy tithe.

Pattern Twelve
The "We've Never Done It That Way"
Syndrome

The Automatic Resistance Response
(Numbers 14:8-10; 1 Corinthians 1:10; Hebrews 13:17)

One of the most common spiritual hindrances could be summed up as the "automatic resistance response." Without question, we all have at least some natural resistance to change. Yet with some, virtually any change is met with angry resistance. Even when there is absolutely no biblical basis for opposition, problem personalities will attempt to frame their objections in scriptural terms (though the objections are not really scripturally based). This is especially sad because change is often a vital part of spiritual growth. Without change, we get stuck in the past and see little progress either corporately or personally. Perhaps this is why *"we have never done it that way before"* has been called the last seven words of a dying church!

The truth is significant growth almost always occurs outside our "comfort zones." When we are determined to stay in our comfort zones and "keep everything the same," spiritual stagnation is virtually assured! Actually, the pattern of change resistance is one of the most serious barriers to God's activity in modern churches. Until churches are willing to embrace the challenges of spiritual change, they are almost certain to decline and eventually die. If you doubt this, consider a sobering fact. At present, somewhere between seventy to eighty percent of American churches are either plateaued or fast declining. Clearly something needs to change!

The "we've never done it that way" syndrome causes

enormous grief and hindrance to God's Kingdom and to His leaders. Those who automatically resist change often find themselves opposing the work of God Himself. (Yet they are usually fairly oblivious to how much they are profoundly hindering God's Spirit.) At its heart, this attitude is one of enormous selfishness and insensitivity. When we adamantly insist on having everything just like we want it, we're basically saying we don't care what others want or need. In essence, we are saying "we don't care about growth or reaching more people, we just want everything to stay in our comfort zone." Little is more damaging to the Church or the Kingdom of God!

Dear reader, have you been guilty of selfishly resisting change? Have you made your personal preferences equal to scriptural laws? Do you view those with different tastes as automatically evil and fleshly? Have you allowed your personal preferences to create bitter anger and division in the Church? In truth, little could be more wrong than to split a church over changes that are less than fundamental. Let us determine to embrace the maturity to keep relatively minor issues from become major battles.

Pattern Thirteen
The Church Hopping
"Jump and Run" Side-Step

(John 13:34-35; 17:21; 1 Corinthians 12-14;
1 John 2:19)

Another common condition is the "jump and run" attitude of more and more church members. I call this pattern the church hopping "side-step" because it enables some believers to side-step the responsibility and spiritual challenge of developing meaningful fellowship with other believers. This pattern also allows people to avoid any real service or responsibility that goes with healthy church membership. Through this method, *believers* can come to "enjoy" the music, programs or preaching yet carefully avoid most or all responsibility. In essence, such members take much and give little. A related and growing pattern is with seniors who retire from work and also retire from serving God. Now that they have more time to serve God than ever before, they decide to serve Him less. Any of these patterns are the very opposite of the biblical picture for mature, responsible church membership. (1 Corinthians 12-14; Ephesians 4:10-12)

A similar unbiblical pattern is the "let's just move on" syndrome. While there are certainly times when God leads believers to change churches, many must later confess it was more from human reasoning than true spiritual guidance. Rather than making deep commitments to a local church, modern believers often play the unbiblical game of musical chairs with their membership. To God, church membership is a solemn commitment to deep, lasting relationships with a certain body of believers. Yet instead of embracing mature fellowship and service, for many believers it is all about *them*, not the body of Christ.

The "Me" Generation

Church hopping has become an enormous problem in today's congregations. So many have the "picky shopper" mentality in deciding on a church. Rather than asking, "How can I serve this church," it is all about how can *I* be served. Unfortunately, so many modern saints look for a church exactly the way they would a health club — they want one with the least cost and most benefits! Often when the least thing becomes disagreeable, people immediately shop for another church. These patterns reflect little concept of a long-term commitment to meaningful relationships or self-less service. Unfortunately, it also suggests little concept of biblical fellowship or mature commitment to Christ.

A major sign of Christian maturity is when believers learn to work and grow *through* their times of relationship challenges. Sooner or later we all face relationship challenges in virtually any church. Especially at these times, God offers us grace to learn to love, forgive and grow, not quickly cut and run. Without question, it is God's will that believers learn how to love and unite in spite of differences. Yet with so many, the attitude is "If you don't do everything I want, I'll just take my marbles and leave." Many even use the *threat* of leaving to try and force their will on others. Needless to say, such attitudes bear no resemblance to Christian love and maturity.

When believers quickly attempt to cut ties and "move on" without thoroughly addressing damaged relationships, *they* may move on but the Holy Spirit doesn't! While we may sever relationships or change churches, we can never again know God's rich fullness and blessing until we give and receive true forgiveness. (Matthew 5:23;6:14) In terms of anger, bitterness and division, what is in the past is *not* in the past if it remains unresolved in our hearts.

Again let us acknowledge that God definitely leads some people to change churches. It is not our place to judge what is in the hearts of others. For each of us, the goal is to be utterly honest with ourselves and with God. Yet, it is vital that modern saints again come to view church membership the way God views it — a sacred, generally lasting commitment to mature fellowship and responsible service with a particular body of believers. To follow Christ, we simply must step up to the plate of mature service and giving to our church. Only by so doing can we glorify God and experience sweeping revival in our day. It is a major red flag when people say things like, "We've been looking for a church where we can just attend and *enjoy* ourselves but not really be involved." That pattern bears no resemblance to the call God gives to all true followers of Christ.

Without question, we are all saved to serve not to sit. A popular phrase once used for our country would surely apply as well to our Savior's Church: "Ask not what your church can do for you but what you can do for your church." Let us now resolve to become givers and servers more than sitters and takers.

Pattern Fourteen
Disrespect of Committees
and Lay-leaders

(Romans 12:9a; Ephesians 4:3;16-18;
Colossians 3:8;12-15)

While not directly against pastor and staff, another common attack is toward church committees who are assigned challenging tasks. Some of the more common targets of attack are building, finance, nominating and pastor search committees. These tasks are especially complex and require extensive deliberation and study. In many cases, committees are required to make decisions that cannot possibly please everyone. Unless there are extreme and obvious reasons to do otherwise, churches must respect the committee process and allow them to do their work. Especially when hard decisions must be made, everyone should make a strong effort to guard the bond of peace and refrain from demanding their own way.

A related attack occurs when some want the pastor search or personnel committees to move faster or in a certain direction. As a general rule, patience and prayerfulness are God's directives. Mature believers will not badger or pressure committees toward a certain end or time frame. Without prayer and maturity, churches can easily divide in times of decision or change. Yet with prayer, patience and maturity, almost any decision can be traversed effectively. May God teach us the maturity and patience to respect one another and resist demanding, selfish attitudes.

Pattern Fifteen
Personalities and Politics
Over God and Kingdom

(Acts 5:29; 1 Corinthians 1:10;3:1-3;
1 Thessalonians 5:12-13)

Closely related is the tendency for some members to be against calling new staff or other decisions simply because they oppose the pastor or committee that recommended them. Though they may not have a thing against the particular person or position, they perceive key church leadership is for it so they are automatically against it. The same thing often occurs with church decisions or new programs. In essence, people with an angry, bitter spirit are opposed simply because the pastor or certain committees are for it. In most cases, they have not seriously sought God's face — they are just blindly against whatever the leadership wants. While they may "say" they have reasons for opposition, the truth is they just don't like who proposed the course of action. If someone they supported had proposed the action, they would have been all for it.

This condition is especially harmful because it often brings people into direct opposition to the vital purposes of God Himself. The Lord will not forever tolerate such serious and willful hindrances to His work. Yet for balance, let me clearly state that pastor and committees *should* be opposed if they are clearly wrong biblically. (And sometimes they are indeed wrong.) However, when opposition to church leadership is mostly from anger or stubbornness, we find ourselves literally resisting God Himself. Concerning resisting God, we should all remember a vital truth — God loses no battles!

84

Another real but subtle form of this condition occurs when believers do not stand for what is clearly right because it would mean disagreeing with friends or family. Yet when something or someone is obviously wrong, believers will then make a choice as to who is really first in their life. If they choose friends or family over God, it could only be termed idolatry. When we place anything or anyone ahead of obeying Christ, it is a blatant form of denying Christ. (If anyone thinks this is in any way over-stated, all they need do is read the clear words of Jesus in Luke 14:26-33.) Some churches (and people) completely lose God's blessing because key members place the approval of people over standing for something that is obviously right. While it is certainly difficult to stand against people we love, the alternative is to deny and disobey Christ. When we follow that path, no one wins and everyone loses. Worse yet, we utterly betray our Savior and His Church.

A related form is when believers try to simply remain neutral and take no stance at all. Yet, almost no one can truly remain neutral! To refuse to stand for God's will is to allow evil to triumph. Many a church has lost God's blessing because believers chose to remain silent when they should have taken a stand. Countless pastors or church leaders have made challenging stands for truth only to find themselves standing alone. Key leaders were conspicuously and *shamefully* silent.

In many cases, simply remaining silent is among the most harmful ways we betray Jesus and His Church. Many a divisive church battle has occurred because members took the easy way and "just didn't want to get involved." *Thousands of believers and churches may never know revival or full blessing until they go back and seek forgiveness for refusing to stand for Christ or His servants!* May God grant us the courage and love to stand for Jesus no matter the cost.

The Power of Reconciliation Services

One of the most encouraging trends is for believers and churches to conduct some form of reconciliation meeting to resolve past offenses. While the various groups are not required to dredge up or resurface old arguments, they are required to fully forgive from the heart. The goal is not necessarily to try and assess who is right or wrong but for all to acknowledge and repent of wrong attitudes or words. While split churches do not have to physically reunite, past bitterness must be forgiven. (However in some cases, churches have actually reunited.)

Whether such reconciliations are done in an official service or just believers who meet privately, the results are often phenomenal! The fact is, many believers and churches will never fully heal or go forward without just such meetings. Let no reader be discouraged — God will surely give you guidance and grace to obey!

Pattern Sixteen
Unfair Comparisons and
"Good Old Days" Fixations

(1 Corinthians 3:3-6; 1 Thessalonians 5:12-13;
1 Timothy 5:17)

*Still another damaging pattern is against pastors, staff or lay-
leaders who follow a long-term or well-loved former leader.*
As believers, we simply must understand that every leader
is unique and we should avoid negative comparisons. All
leaders have their own strengths and weaknesses, so we
must accept that reality. In fact, God usually guides us to
a new leader because there *are* changes we need to make.
We should be ready to change and resist the temptation of
over-comparison and unrealistic expectations. Changes and
growth are seldom easy and we must not complicate the
process by immaturity or over-comparisons.

An unfair attack comes from overly nostalgic attitudes
and "good old days" fixations. In today's fast-changing society, circumstances both in and around churches are always
in transition. When the area around a church is rapidly
growing, that church is infinitely more likely to grow and
have an atmosphere of excitement. The truth is, plain physical circumstances and locations have far more to do with
most modern church growth than we might like to admit.
Churches in these settings often have higher percentages of
children and youth which understandably mean far higher
baptisms. These demographic conditions also help create a
natural sense of excitement, progress and easy success.

Naturally when the area surrounding a church plateaus
or declines, congregational dynamics become very differ-

ent. While churches in such areas can certainly still grow, it becomes much harder and requires far more human effort and real power from God. Yet church members often fail to recognize these realities fully. Consequently, they begin to blame their staff and treat them with less respect because things are "just not like they were when old so and so was here."

Fairly Assessing the Past and Present

Without a full and honest assessment of current church factors, it is easy to give far too much credit to past leaders and way too much blame on those in the present. In many cases, such attitudes are utterly unfair and just plain wrong. In fact, if a church setting is not an "easy grow" expanding area, you should appreciate the leaders who are willing to serve in your harder setting. In many ways, these leaders certainly need (and perhaps deserve) your appreciation, encouragement and support far more than those in much easier, fast-growing areas.

A similar pattern is impatience with young or inexperienced ministers who simply need time to develop and grow. The horrific damage some churches have done to young, inexperienced ministers is beyond words to describe. Because of the brutal unkindness of some churches, countless young ministers and staff have been permanently wounded or even left the ministry entirely. Today's shocking statistics of ministerial burnout suggest serious mistreatment on the part of many churches.

Today there is even a disturbingly high incidence of minister's children dropping out of church when they reach adulthood. One of the main reasons stated is the fact they have seen such outrageous pettiness and loveless behavior from "church members," they want no part of such an organization. It is truly heart-wrenching to witness the lasting damage visited upon many a minister's wife and children. Make no mistake — those responsible for such pain will be held to fearsome accountability before God, unless they fully repent. (Psalm 105:15; Hebrews 13:17)

Dear reader, do you sense any unfair criticism in your own heart or church? Have you been guilty of overly praising past leaders while unfairly condemning those who currently serve? Very little discourages God's servants or hinders Christ's kingdom like a critical atmosphere at church. We all need encouragement and we all need to encourage others. Certainly none of us are perfect and there are always things for which we could pick each other apart. But such attitudes are the exact opposite of Christ's heart. May God teach us the vital importance of tenderhearted love and patience with fellow believers.

Pattern Seventeen
"The Congregational Cold War"

(Matthew 5:23-24; 6:14-15; John 13:34-35; 17:21;
Acts 2:1, 42-47; Romans 15:5-7; Colossians 3:12-15;
1 Peter 1:22)

By most indications, the modern Church is in the midst of unprecedented bickering, division and tension. In fact, one estimate suggests over seventy percent of our churches are either in a major fight right now, just concluding one or about to head into another! Little could more displeasing to our Lord or damaging to the spread of the gospel. Virtually nothing grieves God's Spirit or blocks evangelistic power like anger and unresolved tension among believers.

In the face of so many congregational battles, a uniquely damaging condition has developed in near epidemic numbers. Countless thousands of churches have now settled into what I call the *"congregational cold war."* This condition exists when believers have mostly ceased outward battles, but they neglected to deal with strained relationships. The condition also occurs in churches that may have never fought outwardly but still have serious unresolved issues between members. Unfortunately, they try to bury their grievances and just "move on." Yet, when real relational damage has occurred, it is both ineffective and unbiblical to simply ignore it. (Matthew 5:23-6:14) While "let's just move on" may sound good, to move on without forgiveness and at least attempted reconciliation is utterly contrary to God's commands and principles.

When church members attempt to bury or ignore damaged relationships, at least five distinct patterns become evident. Any one of the five profoundly grieves God's Spirit. It is incredible how unaddressed walls between members create an atmosphere of tension and coldness in a whole church. Prayerfully assess whether there are significant patterns of any of these five in your church. And even if you sense several negative patterns in your church, do not be discouraged. *Over the years, I can tell of apparently hopelessly divided churches which came to truly miraculous healing!* My friend, our God is the God of the impossible and nothing is too hard for Him! (Jeremiah 32:17,27)

Five Tell-Tale Signs of a Church in "Cold War"

(1) *Church members basically retreat to common corners and mostly associate with a little clique that shares their feelings.* While still members of the same church, the various groups purposely have little to do with the other. This is seen in small home fellowships as well as who sits with whom at large church events.

(2) *Some members barely speak to certain other members and actually plan their movements so as not to encounter them.* They will literally go out of their way to avoid a particular part of the building where certain people tend to gather.

(3) *Some members give the pastor, staff or other members the "cold shoulder" treatment.* When they get in a setting where they have to speak or shake hands, they are cool, and make little or no eye contact. As visitors come to the church, they instantly detect a sense of coldness.

(4) *Certain members find it difficult to say anything positive about some people or church programs (no matter how well*

things may be going). Because they are miffed in one area, they tend to be aloof and uncomplimentary about all areas. In other words, they are more or less "sulled up" or in a "spiritual pout."

(5) *Members become withdrawn and cease to share personal burdens or needs with fellow believers.* When a church body becomes somewhat "formal" and "stiff," God's Spirit is grieved and His power is seriously quenched. Obviously, such patterns virtually destroy the koinonia fellowship that is so crucial to functioning as the people of God.

Clearly these patterns of "congregational cold wars" are the exact opposite of warm, koinonia fellowship so vital to God's activity in a church. Yet today, many believers totally misunderstand both the nature and importance of loving, biblical fellowship. Many seem to think the mere absence of outward fighting is all God requires. They think it is more or less acceptable to be aloof and distant to fellow believers as long as they do not show overt anger or attack. Nothing could be further from the truth! *Koinonia fellowship is not simply the "absence" of outward fighting, it is the "presence" of loving warmth, outgoing kindness and relational closeness.* For this reason, healthy churches have many fellowship activities and continually work at doing things together. They treat love, unity and togetherness with enormous seriousness. These mature believers would far rather lose an argument or not get their way than lose a brother or sister.

Relational Coldness is not an Option!

As followers of Christ, we simply do not have the option of withdrawing warmth and fellowship from other believers. (Except in extreme cases like 1 Corinthians 5:11 where we are *commanded* to withdraw fellowship.) To ignore relational damage is to grieve God's Spirit and destroy the power of your own prayers! (Matthew 6:14; Mark 11:25) Jesus even said we are to do good to those who persecute us. (Matthew 5:44) As believers, God further commands us to love and forgive people "from the heart." (Matthew 18:35) In other words, we must genuinely forgive people, not just "say" we do yet still remain cold and distant.

Dear reader, please be completely honest with yourself and with God. If you sense any of these patterns in yourself or your church, immediately confess these sins. Whatever you do, please do not justify or rationalize these conditions! Do not justify your attitude by the fact "They did it first." Another false justification is, "They're not friendly to me." Remember, you are responsible for *you* no matter what *they* do. Above all, do not be discouraged about your situation. Every believer should know that God will honor even small first steps to address church or family tension. *My friend, please do not think your church is hopeless or too far gone!* After all, no church is perfect and God still works with very imperfect people.

While believers certainly do not agree on everything and there will be times of offense, we must learn to love anyway! We must resolve to love our way *through* times of conflict, offenses or tension. After all, the Christ who lives within us said, "Father forgive them" while He literally hung on the cross. By His indwelling grace, we *can* learn to love and forgive those who offend us. We cannot just "sull up" or give people the cold shoulder. When we embrace this pattern, we hurt ourselves (spiritually) far more than we hurt the objects of our displeasure. When we allow any anger or bitterness to remain in our heart, *we* are the spiritual prisoners and *ours* are the prayers that are hindered. (Matthew 18:32-35; Mark 11:25-26) Furthermore, it is *we* who end up having the heart attacks and strokes from internalized bitterness. Indeed, *we* are the ones who become most depressed and miserable.

My friend, if there are believers with whom you have been cold or distant, immediately confess and forsake this sin. If the matter is a serious offense, then closely follow the instructions of Matthew 18:15 and *go to them in love!* If it is a matter you just need to forgive and let go, then do it. Make it a point to spend some quality time with those who have been distant. Go out of your way to pay friendly visits or do something to bless and serve their needs. Only in this manner do we live as sons and daughters of God. (Matthew 5:45) To do anything less is to play a religious game.

It is astounding to see what often happens when you take the initiative to show kindness to those with whom you have been distant. Again, the greatest revivals do not occur by people going "down" the aisle but "across" the aisle to become right with brothers and sisters.

Pattern Eighteen
Hypersensitive Critics, Hot Tempers
and Holier than Thou Judges

(Proverbs 29:11,20:22; Ephesians 4:31-32;
Philippians 4:8; James 4:11-12)

In many churches, there is a small minority of members whose hypercritical, judgmental attitudes put everyone else on edge. Rather than exhibiting the loving, positive attitudes commanded in Philippians 4:8, they have a negative mind-set of criticism and judgment. Instead of saying a glass is half-filled, they will invariably say it is half-empty! If a discouraging word is to be heard, rest assured that it will come from them. Whereas periodic constructive criticism is both necessary and positive, their criticisms tend to be chronic, destructive and negative.

Perhaps even more damaging are individuals who are quick-tempered and prone to spout angry, critical words. God's Word reserves some of its strongest language for those who have short fuses and little self-control. *"A fool gives full vent to his anger; but a wise man keeps himself under control...Do you see a man who speaks in haste? There is more hope for a fool than for him...An angry man stirs up dissension, and a hot-tempered one commits many sins."* (Proverbs 29:11,20,22) God's Word leaves absolutely no doubt that control of one's temper and tongue is among the very first steps of following Christ. Without question, angry spirits and sharp tongues are clear expressions of fleshly carnality and serious spiritual immaturity. No one walking in the Spirit could consistently exhibit such tendencies.

Furthermore, angry, unloving speech does enormous damage to people and seriously quenches God's activity in a church. Absolutely nothing more hinders God's Spirit or releases the activity of the devil. It is crucial that believers see this pattern for what it is—a serious grieving of the Holy Spirit. No believer should *ever* excuse a short fuse or say, "that's just my personality." Since God is love, a believer should not be known as one who is often prone to blow up at others. Those who have little control over their tempers do untold damage to Christ's Church. Perhaps this is why Jesus was often merciful to prostitutes and thieves yet spoke extremely strong words to the critical, mean-spirited and religiously self-righteous. (Matthew 23:13-27) The Bible is absolutely clear that little is more offensive to God.

The Devastating, Long-Term Effects of Unloving Behavior

Countless thousands have dropped entirely out of church because they witnessed so-called "Christians" behave with obvious anger and malice. Imagine the tragedy of some desperately seeking soul going to church only to see anger, division and ugliness among believers. According to Scripture, this all too common occurrence is nothing less than an *abomination*! (Proverbs 6:16) Only eternity will reveal how many people ended up entirely rejecting Christ because of the unkind attitudes and actions of carnal church members. Their blood shall surely be required of those who so seriously damaged their faith. (Matthew 18:6)

But of all the horrible damage done by unkind church members, by far the worst is visited upon the most precious and vulnerable among us. Without question, unloving attitudes and actions are especially devastating to children, youth and new believers! When they see adults act in anger and harshness, they are often permanently affected in their view of Christ and His Church.

Before anyone expresses an ungodly attitude around a child or young believer, they should long reflect on Jesus' stern warning in Matthew 18:6, "*But if anyone causes one of these little ones who believes in Me to sin, it would be better for him to have a large millstone hung around his neck and to be drowned in the depth of the sea.*" Believers, it is vital that we come to view sin the way God views it. God sees sins of attitude and spirit just as vile as outward sins of the flesh. In many cases, He actually views attitude sins as far worse than sins of the flesh.

When we hear of the critical, nitpicky attitudes of some, we must wonder if they ever read such passages as Ephesians 4:31-32. "*Get rid of all bitterness, rage and anger, brawling and slander, along with every form of malice. Be kind and compassionate to one another, forgiving each other, just as in Christ God forgave you.*" Indeed, we would all do well to often read 1 Peter 4:8-9. "*Above all, love each other deeply, because love covers over a multitude of sins. Offer hospitality to one another without grumbling.*" The fact is, none of us are anywhere near perfect and proper attitudes of love mean we overlook one another's flaws. After all, there are certainly no perfect pastors or laypersons. One is never more like God than where kind and forgiving and never more like Satan than when critical and harsh.

Judge Not Thy Brother!

Closely related to the critical and high-tempered is the *"holier than thou judge."* These are people who tend to view others as "unspiritual" if they do not follow their exact patterns or practices. Prideful judgmental attitudes are subtle and infect all age groups and personality types. Prayerfully consider five primary examples: (1) Those who raise their hands or show emotion in worship may criticize those who don't as spiritually dead or legalistic. Conversely, those who don't show much expression may harshly criticize those who do as overly emotional or doctrinally unsound. (2) People who frequently attend prayer meetings or prayer groups may view those who do not as unspiritual and immature. (3) Those involved in evangelism or outreach may harshly judge those who are not as uncommitted and unspiritual. (4) Those who attend Bible studies and discipleship groups may automatically view those who do not as unspiritual. (5) Those who pridefully tout themselves as "Bible scholars" may become nit-picky and start seeing "doctrinal problems" where no significant issues really exist. In other words, they tend to make doctrinal mountains out of molehills. They get fixated on a particular doctrine or practice and lose all sense of balanced biblical focus. Mature saints are able to recognize which issues are simply not worth the risk of splitting a church or getting distracted (and most issues aren't!).

Disagreeing in Love

We must remember that good and godly people do not always agree on every little issue and there is certainly room for variance on non-essential matters. Indeed a vital part of maturity is the ability to recognize the difference between the essential and the non-essential. Yet some lack the wisdom to keep from driving smaller, non-essential issues into major controversies and divisions that are wholly unnecessary. In other words, they develop some pet doctrine or issue and drive it into the ground. Such patterns badly distract us from the main issues of discipleship, evangelism and missions. Obviously, angry, internal arguments and distractions are exactly what Satan intends!

In 1 Corinthians 12-14, God pictures Christ's Church as having many members with very diverse gifts, needs and strengths. Yet, with all our diversity, we are to "endeavor" to live and work in loving unity. (Ephesians 4:2-3) Indeed, we do not all worship, pray, witness or serve God in exactly the same ways (and neither are we required too!), Christian love and maturity demands that we accept and even value our diversity, not divide and fight over it.

It is wonderful to report a growing remnant of churches is working toward greater unity in spite of differing likes and dislikes. Though some of these believers in churches have fought for years, they are now learning to disagree agreeably. No matter how long you or your church have lived in anger and negativism, it is not too late to change! God can turn the most tension-filled churches and families into pictures of grace and love.

Pattern Nineteen
Decision-Time "Free for Alls"

(Matthew 5:9; 1 Corinthians 1:10;
James 1:5;3:14-18; 1 Peter 4:8-9)

Times of major church decisions are often opportunities for disgusting displays of fleshly anger and petty bickering. In fact, many pastors, staff and lay-leaders feel a wave of pure dread when it comes to proposing major projects or calling new staff. From painful experience, they realize how quickly people can become angry and divided. When churches come to times of decision, Satan immediately starts probing for possible ways to bring anger, division and distraction to the church.

Make no mistake — our enemy is always searching for ways to disrupt unity, damage the bond of peace and distract believers from evangelism and missions. Unfortunately, he usually knows exactly where to go to find a willing instigator. In many churches, there are certain people always ready to quickly (and quite loudly) voice an opinion without careful prayer and thorough deliberation. No doubt the primary question to address is *why* major church decisions so easily move into bickering and division. Though certainly there are a variety of reasons, I believe five are most preeminent.

Five Reasons for Decision-Time Church Battles

(1) *Angry divisive bickering is clear indication people are walking in the flesh, not the Spirit.* According to dozens of passages, angry division and bitter strife are the distinct, tell-tale fruits of immaturity and carnality. (1 Corinthians 3:1-3; Galatians 5:19-21; James 3:14-16)

When the Holy Spirit is in charge, believers can make decisions and discuss significant differences with love, maturity and respect. Yet, when people are not yielded to God, selfish attitudes and angry divisions are the order of the day. Fleshly people can and do fight over even the smallest of issues. If several people are exhibiting fleshly attitudes, the church should strongly consider postponing any decisions and go through a period of spiritual cleansing.

(2) *Divisive bickering occurs when believers fail to carefully and prayerfully examine all facts before they form opinions and start promoting them to anyone who will listen.* In today's Church, it is astounding how many people start spouting opinions before they ever even hear the whole project or its reasons. So often, they have not practiced even a modicum of prayer and fasting, yet start loudly proclaiming their opinions. In truth, God's opinion is the only one that matters and we find His will only by deep prayer and meditation, not fleshly reasonings. Yet some people are so arrogant, they think they don't need special time in deep prayer to fully discern God's mind. Obviously, individuals with such attitudes often have little real connection with the heart and mind of God. (1 Corinthians 2:10-16)

(3) *Leaders or committees may indeed be proposing something that is not well advised, well-timed or properly researched.* In other words, they may be proposing something that is simply wrong. A related problem is the fact their presentations may be unclear and incomplete. Leaders or committees may also present a matter at the *wrong time* or in an *improper manner!* Wise leaders know it is

often as important to know the *how* and *when* of God's leadership as the *what*.

(4) *Some people so love controversy and politics, they turn decisions into a "contest" of who can get their way.* By politicking and manipulations, they may attempt to swing the vote. They often don't even realize the real source of their objection. For many, times of decision become key opportunities to settle old scores. If someone has anger toward a pastor or other leader, they may be opposing their proposal as a subconscious way to get even. Though they may not even realize it, some people oppose a project simply because they don't like those who proposed it!

(5) *Satanic opposition is a major causative factor in the anger and bickering surrounding many decisions in church.* In most major church decisions, Satan has a definite stake in how it turns out. Especially if a proposed step has great potential to expand God's kingdom, it would be surprising if Satan didn't oppose it. Satan's primary means of hindering and opposing God's purpose is to stir up those who will listen to his voice and spread his suggestions and whispers. Tragically, those being used by Satan usually have no idea they are tools in his hands. In most cases, they are following human reasoning instead of direction from God's Spirit. While they may truly believe they are fighting for the right thing, the enemy has deceived them into opposing the very purposes of God.

Though satanic influence can certainly be a factor, we must be careful not to judge people who disagree as "speaking from Satan." We must remember that God alone can fully see into hearts and godly people can honestly disagree without one being the voice of the devil. In great humility we must *all* ask God to guard our own hearts from deception and pride. Except in the most extreme or obvious of cases, we must also remain non-judgmental as to other people's motives for opposition. Again, respectful discussion of varying viewpoints is good, not evil. In fact, such prayerful discussions and deliberations are usually how we come to a fuller understanding of the whole will of God. In other words, we *need* each other's reasonable impressions and thoughts.

Four Simple Biblical Rules to Healthy Church Decisions

While the potential reasons for division may seem overwhelming, they are easily overcome by God's grace. *Four simple biblical guidelines will solve most problems in decisions.*

(1) If leaders approach their tasks with thorough deliberation and fervent prayer, God will surely guide them to right proposals.

(2) If lay-people are swift to hear, slow to speak and fervent in prayer, they will receive clear wisdom concerning God's will.

(3) If everyone asks for God's protection from deception and patiently awaits His timing, the decision time will become glorious moments of united growth, not division.

(4) In those areas we still disagree, love teaches us to *disagree agreeably*. May God give us the determination to approach decisions in humility, prayer and thoroughness,

not anger, fleshly reasoning or haste. Indeed, many a battle can be defused by simply putting a decision on hold to enter a period of intense prayer and further deliberation.

A Final Thought on Church Decisions

One of the most important things to remember about times of decision is simply this — most decisions are not worth dividing a church! Except in cases of fundamental doctrine or practice, we must carefully avoid dividing or fighting over smaller issues. In Scripture, we are commanded to "diligently keep the peace." (Ephesians 4:3) In other words, it is often better to keep peace than to cause an argument by angrily demanding our way on non-essential issues.

Another important principle is to simply "let it go" once a church decision is embraced. To continually complain or stir the pot is one of the most immature and spiritually damaging practices a believer can commit. (See Pattern Ten) Again, we must realize that we cannot always get our way and we must humbly accept the church decision and move on.

Pattern Twenty
Relational Brushfires and
Molehill Mountains

(Matthew 5:9; John 17:21; 1 Corinthians 1:10;3:1-3;
James 4:22-12;5:9)

In today's Church, a common problem is the fact so many pastors and lay-leaders are exhausted from constantly dealing with relational brushfires in the congregation. In many churches, there is also a tragic tendency for some to make "mountains out of molehills." Leaders can hardly focus on kingdom matters for having to referee controversies and disputes that should never even arise in the first place.

One of the most damaging effects of brushfires and molehills is what I call the "*drain effect.*" When leaders must constantly deal with "so-called" crises, they lose precious energy and vision for things that really matter. If Satan can thus get leaders distracted, disillusioned and emotionally drained, the work of God is enormously hindered. His predominate method of achieving this end is the willing complicity of people in the church. And very often, these dear saints do not even realize they are being used. With most, their harm to God's work is truly not intentional.

Unfortunately, issues for potential brushfires and molehills are virtually endless. If people are so inclined, there are innumerable issues about which to fight or grumble. We must also realize that one man's molehill is another man's mountain. Thus, a huge part of maturity is the ability to recognize the difference between the *essential* and *nonessential.* While it is certainly appropriate to share our concerns, feelings or preferences with fellow believers, we must do so with love and proper perspectives. With nonessential issues, love demands that we all show much flexibility and consideration for the feelings of others (not angrily demanding our own way). The next section outlines some of the most frequent points for petty, unnecessary bickering.

Common Examples of Potential Brushfires and Molehills

(1) *Hymns or choruses, traditional or contemporary* — It is actually possible for some believers to become so demanding for their own music preference, they strongly criticize leaders simply for including a variety of other styles. Rather than considering the worship leaders' direction or the preferences of other believers, they refuse to give an inch. They have no interest in allowing a mix of styles; they want it all their way. We should note this selfishness and intolerance occurs as much (or more) with the young as with seniors. When attitudes of immaturity are present, the stage is set for continual brushfires on a variety of issues.

(2) *To clap or not to clap in church* — Some people create problems by turning personal preferences like clapping or not clapping into serious biblical injunctions. Yet it is a great mistake to make a big deal about something when the Bible does not. Generally speaking, where the Bible issues no injunctions, neither should we. After all, who are we to judge the inner motivation of "why" someone claps in approval or agreement?

(3) *Music or no music* — Believe it or not, some have actually fought over whether or not to have soft instrumen-

tal music during a Lord's Supper observance. Again, we should never make an issue of something that is clearly not an issue in Scripture.

(4) *We shall not be moved* — Some people would literally rather fight than give up their favorite classroom to classes that need it more. Such attitudes are tragically different from the humble, sacrificial patterns of New Testament Christians.

(5) *We shall not be divided* — When classes need to be divided for growth or fairness to other age groups, some will actually threaten to leave the church.

(6) *Possessiveness and territorialism* — Some become instantly angry when simply asked to alter their ministry assignments. Others are hypersensitive about overlapping responsibilities with other committees. Rather than working together in love and maturity, they become territorial and competitive. Some people are hypersensitive about anyone's work that crosses into "their" area.

(7) *Feelings on sleeves* — In far too many cases, people become angry if others seem to receive more appreciation or attention. Wrongly-motivated, immature people are quickly upset at the smallest perceived criticism or slight. If they are asked to alter or improve something, they are immediately defensive and offended. At the drop of a hat, they are ready to attack others, quit their position or leave the church.

(8) *Self-appointed overseers and unsolicited supervisors* — Some people seem to think it is their life calling to provide a running commentary on the way everyone else does their work in church. They are always telling

anyone who will listen how *they* would do it different. If such comments should ever be made at all, they should be made only after much prayer and only to the appropriate leaders. Self-appointed critics and supervisors do enormous damage to the spiritual atmosphere of a church.

(9) *Hyper-legalists and modern-day Pharisees* — While effective church policies and rules are certainly important, some churches have by-laws that make IRS forms look simple. And rather than applying rules with a spirit of love and grace, some become harsh and condescending. When churches become overly nitpicky and legalistic, hurt feelings and disunity are bound to flourish. It was to harsh legalistic people that Jesus directed the descriptive phrase, *"they strain at a gnat but swallow a camel."* In other words, some people become so angry and rigid about every little rule, that they completely lose sight of loving-kindness and grace (which is the rule of all rules!)

(10) *Rules are for others* — While some drift into hyper-legalism about rules, others want no rules at all. These individuals truly have a defiant, rebellious spirit and a real problem with authority. To them, rules are "meant to be broken." Their inner attitudes toward other believers are, "Who are you to tell me what to do?" People with this fleshly attitude consistently ignore church policies and cause enormous problems in churches. Obviously, such attitudes are utterly inappropriate and create fertile ground for relational brushfires and tension.

(11) *You're in My Pew* — We often hear people jokingly refer to a certain pew as being "theirs." Yet with some

people, there is only one problem—they are not joking! Though it sounds unbelievable, there have been more than a few cases of visitors being given a very hard look when they unknowingly sit in someone's favorite spot. In some instances, they are even sternly told to get up and move. Imagine the absurdity of someone coming to church seeking God, only to be treated rudely concerning where they sit. It is hard to conceive of anything more ridiculously petty, immature, or out of touch with God's heart.

(12) *Temperature Tantrums* — Still another occasion for pettiness on display are angry battles over temperature preferences. While there is certainly nothing wrong with people letting leaders know if they are seriously cold or hot, there is everything wrong with being excessively demanding or unkind. Yet some seem unaware that we all have different preferences and a church has to avoid extremes in either direction. In other words, we all may at times have to dress warmer or cooler if our preferences are out of the middle range. But sadly enough, some refuse and actually threaten to stop attending church if their exact demands are not met. We must wonder what God thinks of those so quick to abandon church when believers in some countries risk their very lives to attend in places with no heat, air or even furniture. If the early church had taken the attitude of some modern believers, it would never have survived the first century. May God help us keep an eternal perspective.

As stated at the beginning, potential issues for brushfires and molehills are almost endless. When people are selfish and overly sensitive, almost anything quickly becomes a major issue. Yet in most cases, one simple principle prevents these damaging distractions—*basic spiritual maturity and placing the needs of others above our own.* (1 Corinthians 3:3; Philippians 2:4)

For balance, let me again say this section is *not* intended to suggest believers should never share their concerns, feelings or preferences to other believers. When done in love and humility, we can certainly share concerns and problems without creating brushfires or mountains out of molehills. In fact, we *should* share significant concerns and needs. Yet, when *non-essential* issues start becoming angry chronic battles, believers must step back, pray up and ask God to help us grow up into loving maturity.

Pattern Twenty-One
Over-Extended Pastors
and Unbiblical Expectations

(Acts 6:2-4; 1 Corinthians 12-14; Ephesians 4:11-12;
1 Thessalonians 5:12-13; 1 Timothy 5:17;
Hebrews 13:17)

Unscriptural and unrealistic job expectations have become enormous hindrances to the effectiveness of many modern pastors. While this pattern is largely unintentional, the damage is nonetheless profound. When pastors and lay leaders are expected to assume so many non-essential roles, they have little time to focus on the "main" things. In Acts 6:2-4, we find the clear biblical pattern for the essential focus of preachers. *"So the Twelve gathered all the disciples together and said, It would not be right for us to neglect the ministry of the Word of God in order to wait on tables. Brothers, choose seven men from among you who are known to be full of the Spirit and wisdom. We will turn this responsibility over to them and will **give our attention to prayer and the ministry of the Word.**"*

In today's Church, most congregations have expectations of pastors that are very different from the clear patterns of Scripture. Unrealistic job expectations cause enormous diversion of pastors' energies. If the pastor is expected to be present for every tiny illness, attend all meetings and guide every committee, when can he spend the major time in prayer and Scripture study so necessary to be a highly anointed preacher and teacher of the Word? If he is consumed by far too many roles (that others really should be doing) when does he pray, win souls or hear God's full vision for the church? *The answer is he doesn't!* Because he is divided by so many roles, he often cannot preach in dynamic power, hear God's vision or win large numbers to Christ. Because of excessive, unbiblical expectations, huge portions of his time are consumed on issues of lesser eternal impact. When this occurs, pastors are seldom able to lead churches into powerful revival and kingdom growth. It is a classic example of the "good" becoming the enemy of the "best."

We Will Give Ourselves to the "Word of God and Prayer"

While pastors must certainly perform effective administration, visitation and ministry to the sick, they cannot be expected to do it all (especially when illness and needs are relatively minor). In reality, mature church members would not really want their pastors to take precious time from critical eternal matters to give them unnecessary attention. Furthermore, God's Word clearly shows the "whole church body" as ministering one to another. (Romans 12:3-8; 1 Corinthians 12-14) It plainly shows the minister's role as primarily giving himself to the "*Word of God and prayer for the equipping of the saints.*" (Acts 6:2-4; Ephesians 4:12)

When the pastor's role becomes excessive and overextended, essential kingdom work invariably suffers. In this unbiblical pattern, church members are deprived of developing their gifts and pastors have little time for the most crucial kingdom issues. Pastors become exhausted from overwork and church members become spiritually stale and weak from inaction. This pattern is a perfect prescription for weak churches, exhausted ministers and idle, immature church members who seldom use their spiritual gifts.

A Satanic Strategy for Weak Churches and Burned-Out Pastors

In Ephesians 6:11, Paul describes the devil as an evil adversary with elaborate schemes to harm believers and hinder Christ's work. Indeed, a master plan of Satan is to get churches (and pastors) structured in ways that are unbiblical and inefficient. In fact, unbiblical and excessive expectations of pastors are among Satan's most effective tools. Today, unprecedented numbers of pastors are leaving the ministry from exhaustion and burnout. Studies show more and more pastors are exhausted, burned out and dying early from stress-related illnesses. What is happening to modern pastors and staff is unprecedented and devastating to kingdom work. In today's ministry patterns and philosophies, something is clearly wrong!

For balance, let me stress that few churches purposely abandoned biblical patterns of leadership. Subtle changes slowly evolved over several decades until churches finally reached today's patterns. Yet concerning these patterns, there is at last indication of positive change! More and more churches desire a pastor who is truly an anointed prophet, shepherd and spiritual leader. These churches do not expect their pastor to visit everyone who has a slight illness or lead every committee. While he certainly attends to those in real need, he is expected to spend much time in prayer and study to lead the church into revival and powerful evangelism.

Before some churches even call a new pastor, they are asking their members to step up to the plate of ministry. They are thus freeing their pastor for greater focus on issues of higher kingdom impact. Members are asked to stop expecting the pastor to attend to their every tiny ache or pain. These churches are not only freeing him for greater kingdom focus, they *expect* it. It should come as no surprise these are the churches seeing dynamic growth and health.

I wish I could report that most churches have moved more toward leadership patterns of the New Testament. (Acts 6:2-4; Ephesians 4:12) Tragically, the vast majority still expect pastors to try and be all things to all members. Self-centered members continue to attack pastors for the pettiest of so-called slights. No doubt, such immaturity is a huge reason many churches never see revival, vibrant health or explosive evangelism.

Yet to God's praise, there is a last some good news to report! Growing numbers are returning to more biblical ministry expectations for pastors and lay leaders. May this trend continue until revival again sweeps our land! For help on biblical ministry philosophies, check out three related resources. (1) *Vital Spiritual Principles for Pastors Search Committees: Seeking God before Seeking a Pastor.* (2) *Restoring the Missing Elements of Revived Churches* and (3) *Seven Essentials of Holiness and Power in Christian Leaders.* All these books are available through the Baptist General Convention of Oklahoma at nominal costs.

Pattern Twenty-Two
Prayerless Programs and
Change for the Sake of Change

(Joshua 9:14; Proverbs 14:12; Jeremiah 10:23;
1 Corinthians 12-14; James 1:5)

While change is an important part of growth, certain members can become overly restless and push toward "change for the sake of change." Because some other church did something, they may become insistent on immediately embracing that exact plan. Some groups may put enormous pressure on leaders to quickly make major changes in certain patterns or practices.

We also live in a day of unprecedented proliferation of new formulas, programs and theories on how to "do church." While some are clearly biblical and blessed of God, not all that is new or popular is right for every church. Unfortunately, some programs have in their structure very little prayer and virtually *no* spiritual cleansing of participants. No program or formula should be allowed to become a substitute for either fervent prayer or seeking God's unique direction and timing for each church. While proposed changes can often be God-led and positive, churches must resist four common mistakes that can cause enormous damage.

Four Common Mistakes in Church Changes

(1) *We must resist the pressure to make changes without carefully seeking God's specific leading for our particular congregation.* It is important to realize that every church and community is unique. God is generally not into "cookie cutter patterns" which suggest all churches are supposed

115

to be nearly identical. Some may read the latest approach and start pressuring leaders to immediately embrace those exact changes. Because some church down the road did something they assume it must be God's will for us. Yet because every church has uniquenesses in age makeup, history, setting and vision, each must find and follow God's specific guidance. Churches must get their primary direction from *God*, not just men or pre-programmed strategies. (Joshua 9:14; Proverbs 14:22)

(2) *We must resist the pressure to make changes that may be right in content or theory but wrong in method and timing.* In some churches, dramatic change can happen quickly and smoothly while in others, the very same approach would create a shipwreck. Following God's will often includes the *how* and *when* as much as the *what*. In other words, it would be far better to take two years to process a change (and keep healthy unity) than force it in six months and split the church! (John 17:21; Ephesians 4:2-3)

(3) *We must resist the unbiblical idea that bloody "transition wars" are simply inevitable and normal.* While some conflict is to be expected in major changes, following God's direction and timing usually brings minimal damage and maximum growth. When it comes to needed change, our Lord is certainly concerned that transitions occur with the greatest possible love and unity. The belief it is acceptable for groups to run roughshod over one another is simply not biblical. With God, it is all about relationships—loving Him and loving each other! (Matthew 22:37-38; John 13:34-35; 1 Corinthians 12-14)

(4) *We must resist the false idea that certain music styles, growth*

formulas or organizational structures are the primary keys to revival and growth. Throughout history, God has sent sweeping revival and explosive evangelism in a vast array of differing worship, preaching and organizational styles. Sweeping revival and kingdom growth are *never* mostly about particular methods or styles! However, in every historic move of God there are three unchanging constants. Revival and New Testament power are always centered around fervent prayer, strong biblical preaching and deep repentance! These are the non-negotiable, essential principles. In other words, God has plan A and there is no plan B. While methodological changes are certainly important and positive, they must never supercede fervent prayer, repentance, discipleship and biblical evangelism (not syrupy, man-centered froth.) As far as empowering His Church, God has always had only one principle! That changeless, eternal principle for empowerment is intense united prayer and deep repentance with relational unity. (2 Chronicles 7:14; Matthew 21:13; John 13:34-35;17:21; Acts 2:1)

If the emphases of the church gets out of balance, we may well find ourselves with bigger crowds but lower commitment, shallow discipleship and declining baptism ratios. Contrary to some philosophies, the goal is *not* simply bigger — *it is bigger with healthy biblical balance!* God's primary goals are always revival and balanced New Testament Christianity, *not* bigger crowds and better entertainment. While several of today's church growth philosophies are very helpful, some are biblically unbalanced. While some short-term numeric growth may indeed occur, the long-term fruit may well be a crop of lost church members and shallow, spectator Christians who never grow to maturity or Christian service.

The Seven Biblical Tests for Healthy Church Changes

As we observe rapid changes in today's Church, it is evident some are good and biblical while others simply are not. We must carefully evaluate all changes by the doctrines and principles of Scripture, *not* by what is merely popular. While some claim "success" from certain changes, the efficacy of any change should always be tested by seven questions.

(1) Are the changes thoroughly biblical in doctrine, balance and principle?

(2) Do we see Christian commitment, discipleship, Bible-focus and spiritual growth moving to a deeper level?

(3) Are the changes moving the church toward far deeper levels of prayer, repentance, holiness and worship?

(4) Are significantly more people being reached through true conversions, evangelism and focus on missions?

(5) Does the church more resemble the New Testament pattern of reaching a diverse culture?

(6) After the initial challenging period of adjustment, will the church become stronger in the bond of peace and loving unity? (In other words, the changes are being approached in a manner and timing that brings the least division and maximum blessing.)

(7) Do these changes make us more or less like the actual doctrines and practices of the New Testament Church? (We should be wary of any changes that keep us from

sharing the "whole council of God" or "watering down" the message?)

In concluding this point, let me again stress that change is a real part of growth! Churches definitely need to adapt and evolve to better reach an ever-changing culture. Toward that end, many of today's changes in worship and approach are very positive and much used of God. Several modern books and strategies are well worth reading and have indeed helped millions. We must all further realize that transition is seldom easy and churches should be thankful for leaders willing to help them adjust to better reach our world. Yet, in all changes we are to remember three vital principles. (1) We must ensure that all changes are absolutely Bible-centered, theologically correct and spiritually balanced. (2 Timothy 3:16) (2) Let everything be done decently and in order. (1 Corinthians 14:40) (3) Let all things be done with the laws of love and unity preeminent. (Matthew 22:38; 1 Corinthians 1:10; Ephesians 4:3) Thank God, His grace is sufficient to help us change and grow without World War Three!

Pattern Twenty-Three
Organizational Maintenance Over
Kingdom-Expansion

(Matthew 6:33;9:37-38;28:16-18; Luke 6:38;14:23)

A most tragic development in today's Church is the strong tendency toward "inward organizational maintenance" over "outward kingdom expansion." This pattern exists when the vast majority of church energies, focus and resources are centered inward rather than outward. When the majority of church activities and focus are upon believers' enjoyment rather than serious discipleship, evangelism and missions, two conditions become pronounced.

First, the Holy Spirit is seriously quenched and grieved because the focus is totally different than that of Christ. Second, the predominantly inward focus produces a sense of luke-warmness and spiritual deadness. I call this condition the "Dead Sea effect." The Dead Sea effect is when churches or people have little or no outlet for significant kingdom-ministry and service. When there is little or no outlet for outward kingdom service, we inevitably become stale, lifeless and self-absorbed. Sadly enough, inward-focused churches exhibit all too familiar patterns.

Seven Characteristics of
Inward-Focused Churches

Churches or people caught in an inward focus exhibit very distinct characteristics. (1) Baptisms tend to be very low and worship service decisions infrequent. In these churches, there is a general lack of God's anointing and power. (2) Planning meetings are mostly about setting calendar and activities, not seeking God's strategic vision for ever expanding ministries. At such meetings, prayer is merely a perfunctory formality at the beginning and end of the session. (3) Church ministries see very little change or development from year to year. Whatever changes do occur, tend to be declines and reductions. (4) Finances tend to be plateaued or declining. In most cases, there are ever-shrinking resources. (5) Conflict and tension over smaller issues is disturbingly common. Inward-focused churches tend to bicker over a wide range of non-essential matters. In general, their focus is more on the temporal than the eternal. (6) Pastor and staff spend far more time on minor needs and organizational maintenance than activities of vital kingdom expansion. In many ways, they are more "managers" than ministers and leaders. (7) Pastor and staff often feel somewhat smothered by a general church attitude of smallness and self-focus. They may often feel more like "caretakers" of a Christian social club than leaders of Christ's victorious Church on mission.

"Majoring on Minors" Breeds Bickering and Conflict

When churches turn inward, it is far more common for members to battle over a wide array of lesser issues. In fact, if some believers exhibited half the passion for evangelism they show over small non-essentials, church baptisms would explode through the roof! Conversely churches that are heavily focused on kingdom expansion and ministry tend to have phenomenal unity and vision. *When we focus on the "main things" we have little time (or inclination) to fight over smaller issues.* Being kingdom-minded has a glorious way of putting things in eternal perspective. People that are Spirit-filled and kingdom-minded simply don't have time to battle over such things as music styles, classroom arrangements or personal preferences.

Concerning this issue, there is good news to report. There is a small but growing trend toward churches seeking to become "kingdom" rather than "inward" focused! Though admittedly, it is still a small minority, kingdom-focused churches are increasing. It is also encouraging to report that *any* small church can embrace kingdom principles. Even churches that are predominately senior adults are finding creative new ways to embrace significant kingdom focus. And when they do, the resulting change is astounding! In these congregations, God's Spirit becomes far more active and bickering much less prevalent. As focus and ministry becomes more outward, the river of God's Presence brings glorious new life and newness. Best of all, I stress that *any* church can learn to be more God-centered and kingdom-focused! No matter what our challenges, God will meet us we are we are and graciously lead us to a whole new level of life and ministry. The results are absolutely miraculous!

Seven Tests for Kingdom-Focused, Revival-Seeking Churches
"Embracing Strategic Visions that Come from God!"

In researching history's Great Awakenings, I have identified seven factors that generally characterize churches in full New Testament power. Indeed, the churches that actually experienced sweeping revival and awakening, typically embraced *seven* key elements, *not* just the four or five common today. Thus, it is indeed possible for a church to evaluate its purpose and vision to determine whether it is in a full revival and kingdom-focus pattern. Any church that is truly kingdom-focused and revival seeking can generally answer yes to seven specific questions. Please prayerfully evaluate your church's practices, priorities and strategic vision based on these key points.

(1) *Do you have a concrete strategy to move your church into God-initiated times of thorough biblical cleansing and repentance in the foreseeable future?* (i.e. solemn assemblies, church-focused revival meetings, a special period of relational cleansing, etc.) Though essential, this principle is strictly as God leads and is not conducted as a program. Churches serious about seeking God and revival are utterly committed to embracing patterns of deep cleansing and repentance.

(2) *Do you have a God-led strategy to greatly increase the personal and corporate prayers and holiness of the congregation?* (i.e. developing intense discipleship in prayer, embracing powerful corporate prayer meetings and corporate repentance, developing evangelistic prayer ministries, family prayer emphases, etc.) Churches serious about seeking God and revival are utterly committed to developing fervent personal and corporate prayer.

(3) *Do you have a God-led strategy to greatly increase personal and group evangelism practices in your church?* (i.e. soul winning training, Sunday School outreach crusades, evangelism projects, etc.) Churches serious about seeking God and revival are utterly committed to evangelism.

(4) *Do you have a God-led strategy to greatly increase personal and corporate missions involvement in your congregation?*

(i.e. emphasizing sacrificial missions giving, missions praying, missions trips and projects, adopting certain countries, etc.) Churches serious about revival are utterly committed to missions.

(5) *Do you have a God-led strategy to greatly increase personal and corporate discipleship patterns in your church?* (i.e. serious discipleship training, discipleship/prayer groups, discipling converts, marriage and family prayer development, etc.) Churches serious about seeking God and revival are utterly committed to ever deepening discipleship.

(6) *Do you have a God-led strategy to greatly deepen church fellowship, guard unity, minister to the Body and heal relationships?* (i.e. strong ministries to sick and needy, effective koinonia fellowship and activities, relationship cleansing processes to deepen unity and heal damaged relationships, etc.) Churches serious about seeking God and revival are utterly committed to deepening koinonia fellowship, internal ministry and loving relational oneness.

(7) *Do you have a God-led strategy to greatly deepen patterns of worship and balanced, biblical preaching?* (i.e. prayerful planning to enhance and develop corporate worship, sending the pastor to conferences for biblical preaching, etc.) Churches serious about seeking God and revival are utterly committed to deepening their corporate worship and ministry of the Word.

Any Church Can Become God-Centered and Kingdom-Focused!

I am thrilled to assure readers that any church can embrace a God-initiated, kingdom-focused vision! Obviously each church would certainly have its own God-guided uniqueness as to which of the seven priorities they devote their focus at any given time. But one thing is certain — *all seven of these areas are vital to bringing a church into true revival and kingdom-focused health!* We cannot afford to be consistently lax or consistently unfocused in *any one* of the seven. For this reason, our strategic planning and vision must specifically address all seven key priorities of God. The good news is, we *can!* Any church could use these seven steps to prayerfully seek God in strategic planning and vision that originates with Him! These seven points enable churches to become highly *focused* and *specific* in obeying God's essential priorities.

Rediscovering the Essential "Relational Triggers" of Revival

Many churches are already to some degree focused on the basic four or five common purposes (though often inadequately). Indeed, we pretty well know to target evangelism, missions, discipleship, fellowship and worship. And yet, the elements that are the actual *"relational triggers"* to revival are almost wholly ignored. **The actual triggers to revival and New Testament power are:** (1) *Intense personal and corporate prayer* and (2) *Deep personal and corporate repentance with special focus to relational unity.* If these two emphases are missing or only lightly emphasized, the power for the other five is greatly diminished. Only an intense focus on fervent prayer, profound cleansing and relational oneness can fully empower the other basic purposes!

If the two relational triggers are neglected, we are reduced to functioning without the full revival power of God. While we can certainly see some blessing, we do not see sweeping revival and spiritual awakening. If anyone doubts the truth of that statement, all one need to do is take an objective look at today's statistics and trends. Have we not been mostly focusing on the basic five purposes for the past fifty years? Have we not seen one new strategy or formula after another? Indeed we have! So what has been the result? We have witnessed by far the worst moral and spiritual collapse in our nation's history! Clearly something *is* missing! Without question, intense united prayer, deep cleansing and loving relational unity *are* the three missing elements! These elements cannot be treated as "side issues" and still maintain the necessary intensity of focus to see either revival or New Testament power. Yet in truth, that is exactly what we have done.

So how about it, dear reader? In your personal and church planning, do you prayerfully consider *all seven* priorities of kingdom-focus? By God's grace, we can all adjust to include the elements so often missing from our focus and planning. It is truly amazing what happens when we become *kingdom* and *revival* focused in our planning and practice! By so doing, we at last begin to seek the Reviver not just revival. When we seek the Reviver, we find all the revival we could ever imagine!

Pattern Twenty-Four
Nay-Saying and Perpetual Doubting

(Numbers 13:27-33;32:7; Matthew 9:29;13:58;
Hebrews 3:12-19)

Of all the vital spiritual principles, expectant faith stands at the very top. In Matthew 9:29, Jesus summarized this principle of enormous eternal importance. *"It shall be unto you according to your faith."* In the gospels, Jesus repeatedly taught that God is at work in and through our lives to the degree we are specifically trusting Him. Powerful, expectant faith is absolutely central to both revival and New Testament ministry. Yet, strong faith has implications even beyond spiritual power. It is the very heart of our love relationship with God!

Faith is not only crucial to spiritual power, it is essential to pleasing God. *"But without faith it is impossible to please Him: for he that cometh to God must believe that He is and that He is a rewarder of them that diligently seek Him."* (Hebrews 11:6) Throughout Scripture and history, God consistently tests His people to see if they genuinely trust Him. In fact, fulfilling a God-given vision nearly always requires genuine courage and faith. Furthermore, a true vision from God is always bigger than humans and requires both faith and patience to see fulfillment. (Hebrews 6:12) If the enemy can persuade us to doubt and give up, the power and blessing of God is seriously blocked. Thus, it is little wonder that Satan's first line of attack is getting believers discouraged and doubting.

For a balanced perspective, let me point out that honest questions, hesitation or opposition to a proposed direction does not necessarily mean doubt. In some cases, a proposed direction is simply wrong and should be opposed. Furthermore, people can honestly disagree about issues or projects without one group being doubters and naysayers! As with the issue of decisions, we should be very careful about judging people as "hindrances" simply because they do not agree on all points. After all, walking in faith does not mean we automatically embrace all projects. Just as unbelief is a serious sin, so is presumption! To charge into a project without God's clear direction and promise is not faith, it is presumptive foolishness. We must clearly understand that God is not obligated to back plans and projects He did not originate. Yet, when a church has definite kingdom-building direction, Satan's number one strategy is to create discouragement and doubt.

So how does the enemy most often damage the faith of individuals and churches? For the most part, it is an "inside job." According to Scripture, his primary tools often involve fellow believers who sow subtle seeds of discouragement and doubt. Persistently negative-minded believers are close spiritual relatives of the Israeli spies who brought a bad report of discouragement and fear. *"And they spread among the Israelites a bad report about the land they had explored. They said, "The land we explored devours those living in it. All the people we saw there are of great size. We saw the Nephilim there (the descendants of Anak come from the Nephilim). We seemed like grasshoppers in our own eyes, and we looked the same to them."* (Numbers 13:32-33)

It is significant that the doubters looked at the land God had promised and saw the size of the obstacles instead of the size of God. They foolishly focused on themselves and their enemies rather than the power and promise of God. Tragically the Israelites listened to the doubters and the result is an object lesson for all generations. And what is that lesson? *Generations, churches or people that consistently doubt, die in the spiritual wilderness!* Dear readers, this sad pattern is rampant in thousands of churches today. When we begin to doubt God, we immediately short-circuit the flow of His presence in our lives and churches. (Matthew 13:58)

When people or churches grieve God's Spirit by unbelief, they are quickly reduced to living by fleshly abilities rather than God's supernatural enablement. As a result, countless thousands live dry, defeated lives with very little power or vision. Year after year, church baptisms remain low while conflict and tension seem ever present. When people or churches fail to live by expectant faith, they live their lives in the spiritual desert! Since God has provided such glorious victory and power, little is sadder than believers and churches settling into the desert of doubt.

An attitude of doubt is also a death knell to church vision. When people doubt God, they seldom receive His vision for either their lives or churches. In Proverbs 29:18(KJV), God leaves little doubt as to the importance of a powerful vision from Him. "*Where there is no vision, the people perish.*" Today it is sad but true that most churches have no specific God-breathed vision for expanding their ministries. If a church is neither attempting nor doing anything unexplainable by human efforts and programs, that church likely has no real vision from God. His visions are usually far beyond the reach of anything but super-natural enablement.

When we consider the devastating results of unbelief, it is little wonder that Satan so feverishly works to cause churches to doubt God. The devil is indeed a master at creating discouragement, fear and negative thinking in congregations. And as with many of his attacks, the devil's most powerful weapon is willing accomplices within the church. While virtually no believer would intentionally become a tool to create doubt, it is nonetheless a very common occurrence. In fact, the Bible contains clear examples of doubt doing its deadly work among believers. In the next section, I briefly describe the primary ways the enemy uses people to foster doubt and defeat churches. Please pause and ask God if any of these sinful patterns are at work in your own life or church.

Five Sources of Doubt Within Congregations

(1) *Doubt often comes through members who think and speak far more through human reasoning than faith in the all-powerful God.* These individuals measure potential much more by human abilities than by God and His promises. While there are many biblical examples of this condition, among the clearest is the ten spies who were assigned to assess the Promised Land for conquest. (Numbers 13:17-20) Yet a tragic thing occurred. When they looked at the land and its challenges, they measured by their own abilities instead of God's omnipotence. Even through God had clearly promised to give them the land, they looked through human reasoning and doubted. They simply did not believe God's promise was also the assurance of His power and provision. Thus they committed the fatal error. When they looked at their challenges, they measured by themselves and said, *"We can't do it."*

Absolutely nothing displeases God more or assures our defeat more than doubt! God loves the "can do" spirit of faith and rejects those who often lean toward unbelief. Furthermore these patterns are especially deadly because doubt and fear are *terribly contagious!* It often only takes a few vocal nay-sayers to discourage and derail a whole church. Only eternity will reveal the glorious opportunities and visions that failed because people listened to voices of unbelief.

(2) *Doubt comes through the unbiblical idea that problems, challenges or setbacks automatically mean we are out of God's will.* Yet in God's Word, we see it is actually quite normal to run into serious problems and challenges in the very center of God's will. Throughout all of Scripture, God's people constantly faced challenges and crises as they followed His path. In fact, trials are the primary way God tests and grows our faith! (Romans 5:1-3) We are even commanded to "*count it all joy when we fall into various trials.*" (James 1:1-4)

We must also remember we are in a raging spiritual war with an enemy who fires real bullets. How could we expect to be in a real war and not encounter great challenges and setbacks? No doubt, this is part of God's meaning when He inspired Peter to write these words. "*Dear friends, do not be surprised at the painful trial you are suffering, as though something strange were happening to you.*" (1 Peter 4:12) Though battles, challenges and problems sometimes do indicate God's displeasure, often they are just a normal part of our journey of faith and spiritual warfare.

While mature saints understand the inevitability of battles, perpetual doubters are always ready to give up and quit. Again, we find a prime example in Israel's wilderness wanderings. Every time they faced a new crisis or need, they panicked and assumed the worst. Whether it was an urgent need for water, food, direction or protection, their reaction was always the same—*we should have stayed in Egypt!* (Exodus 16:3) Does this sound familiar? If churches (or people) are to walk in victory, they must view problems and needs as opportunities to trust and move forward, not doubt and give up! For this reason, those often prone to voice doubts are enormous hindrances to the progress of any church or family.

(3) *Doubt and discouragement frequently come through the "blame the leader syndrome."* When God's people encountered trials, the predictable reaction of some was to blame Moses. To them, difficulties *must* be someone's fault and leaders were the easiest target. Since most people will not come right out and attack or malign God, they target a human leader. Yet the Bible plainly teaches a much forgotten truth. If a leader is sincerely following God's direction, to reject or malign the leader is to reject God! (1 Samuel 8:7)

Unfortunately, this pattern is all too common in the modern Church. The condition is especially damaging because it causes people to get their eyes off God. However, for balance, let me clearly state that leaders are not to be afforded blind allegiance. If they are leading in a way that clearly contradicts Scripture or God's Spirit, we must address it by the patterns of Matthew 18:15. Yet in general, God sends much of His direction and power through His appointed leaders. For this reason, Satan constantly seeks to inspire people to attack, belittle or discourage God's leaders. If someone has a persistent habit of criticizing leaders, there is very little doubt who controls their tongue.

(4) *Doubts may come from a sense of condemnation or inadequate understanding of God's goodness and grace.* Every shred of our faith and confidence is wholly dependent upon God's grace through the blood of Jesus Christ. One thing is certain—none of us *deserve* God's mercy, power or blessing. It is further evident that none of us have achieved perfect holiness in our daily walk. Yet our confidence still rests secure in one great truth—*we are accepted in the Beloved!* (Ephesians 1:6) God is our Emmanuel who will never leave us or forsake us. (Hebrews 13:5). While our loving God must certainly chastise us if we persist in willful sin, He is not an angry God meticulously searching for reasons to judge His children. God's grace is incredible and His goodness higher than the heavens! Because of God's grace, we have every reason to pray and believe for glorious kingdom conquests.

Yet for believers with a mind-set of doubt, their God is small, angry and stingy with His power. They tend to live in fear and condemnation, expecting little beyond average existence. We see such fear in the Israelites' terrified statements, *"He has brought us into the dessert to kill us."* (Exodus 14:11-12) Doubting His goodness, power and grace also gives us a bad case of the *"grasshopper complex."* (Numbers 32) Such attitudes of fear stem either from serious unconfessed sin or a shallow understanding of our covenant of grace. Either way, churches must not let doubters or nay-sayers keep them from vibrant faith and vision. To do so is to "die in the spiritual wilderness."

(5) *Doubt comes from subtle unwillingness to embrace the necessary challenge and spiritual exertion of vibrant faith and vision.* In truth, many prefer the predictability of living in a rut to the challenge of following a God-size vision. It is also true that greater vision brings greater warfare and sacrifice. While the eternal results are well worth the sacrifices, doubters prefer the safety of the harbor to the open sea challenges of a God-size vision.

Indeed some people will discourage and oppose any aggressive project because it will surely mean hard work and financial sacrifice. In many cases, these brothers and sisters are not even aware the real source of their objection. May God grant us the insight and honesty to avoid this vision-killing mind-set. Let us avoid the attitude so tragically expressed by Israel in the desert. Many actually preferred Egypt to the battles and challenges of glorious conquests in Canaan. Thousands of great ministries and dreams "die in the desert" because believers doubt God and love the status quo!

Leaders Even More Accountable!
(James 3:1)

Unfortunately, examples of attacks on churches and leaders are ever increasing. In light of today's disturbing patterns, one thing is certain — before some churches can experience true revival or blessing, they must seek forgiveness from pastors, staff or fellow believers they have mistreated. Many churches also have to ask forgiveness from a former pastor, staff person or lay-leader. *However, let me be clear that in many other cases, pastors, staff or committees must ask the forgiveness of churches or individuals they themselves have wronged.* Unity problems in churches are by no means always the fault of lay-people. In fact, many pastors and staff must pray about ways they may have worsened congregational problems by failing to seek God's full direction, method or timing in church decisions.

When it comes to leading churches, discerning God's *method* and *timing* are almost as important as discerning *what* He wants us to do. In many cases, we (leaders) may need to publicly apologize for careless leadership or immature attitudes toward our laymen. Sometimes we quickly blame laypeople for "not following" when the truth is our leadership timing and methods were simply wrong. Thank God when we humble ourselves and ask forgiveness, glorious healing comes to us and our churches! But until we get honest and admit our own failures, healing and revival virtually never come. Dear leaders, honest and humble confession and repentance must begin with us.

Growing Signs of Hope

After describing these patterns in today's Church, I am delighted to say there are some small but rapidly growing signs of hope! More and more believers are beginning to realize, *"It is impossible to truly love God and not love one another."* To God's praise, we are at last seeing maturity and unity increasing in some churches. Slowly but surely, some churches are finding the love and maturity to deal with cultural and generational differences in a Christian manner. Through

God's grace, love and unity are certainly possible (if we're ready to forsake childish and selfish behavior.) *Thank God, the most divided church can actually become the most united!* Friends, if we are to experience a modern day revival flood, intentional love and unity must again become our priority and practice. (John 13:34-35;17:21)

Another glorious trend is the growing number of churches that are getting right with congregations that formed as a "split" from their own! Again, this does not mean the churches have to physically reunite, but it *does* mean they must fully confess and forgive past offenses. Dear reader, until you attempt to reconcile with those you fought in the past, there *cannot* be full blessing on your church or your life! Remember, until you are prepared to get right with others, your very prayers and worship are seriously hindered before God. (Psalm 66:18; Matthew 5:23;6:14, Ephesians 4:30; 1 Peter 3:7) You can change! Please do not let Satan give you any more excuses! Let God give you His wonderful grace and deliverance.

Conclusion

If you have been honest and thorough in confessing your sins, you are beginning to experience God's full cleansing power. Sins that are admitted and forsaken are fully cleansed. It is important to trust in God's promise of forgiveness, *not* your feelings. (1 John 1:9)

Three basic guidelines are helpful in your confession:

(1) If the sin is against God, confess it to God, and make things right with Him.

(2) If the sin is against another person, confess it to God, and make things right with the other person.

(3) If the sin is against a group, confess it to God, and make it right with the group. (Though you should use discretion not to hurt or slander other people in the process.)

To the degree there is full confession, you will experience full cleansing and glorious transformation. As you confess your sins, ask God to fill you with the Holy Spirit. Do not be discouraged if some sins at first seem difficult to overcome. Some will require a *process* of frequent confession and claiming Christ's fullness. Don't ever give up and don't feel condemned in the process of the battle. If you persist in daily confession and truly trust God for Christ's indwelling power, you *will* experience complete and total victory. Don't ever say you can't change when God's says you can! *"I can do all things through Christ!"* (Philippians 4:19, KJV)

Friend, it is vital that you believe Christ's death and resurrection provides your present victory over sin's *power* as well as its *penalty*. According to Romans 6:6, we are to claim Christ's victory over our sins. As we reject the patterns of sin and self, we then trust Christ to fill us with His own power and righteousness. We can then experience the glorious declaration of the apostle Paul in Galatians 2:20(KJV): *"I am crucified with Christ: nevertheless I live; yet not I but Christ lives in me."*

As you experience this continuing process of cleansing and filling, you will move into a dynamic daily walk with God. Yet, the absolute key is your daily prayer life! God wants every believer to experience a dynamic prayer life. He wants you to walk in spiritual victory and experience miraculous answers to prayer. God wants you to be able to clearly hear His voice and learn how to be a powerful intercessor. He wants to teach you how to daily worship and walk in His continual guidance. But how do you move into such a balanced, biblical prayer life on a daily basis? What are the practical steps? The following points provide a biblical starting place.

Five Practical Steps to a Powerful Daily Prayer Life

1. Make an absolute commitment to consistently spend significant time alone with God in uninterrupted prayer.

It is essential that you begin to give God *significant* time on a daily basis. *Two or three minute devotions are by no means the pattern of Jesus, the early church or anyone mightily used by God.* You must reject the modern notion that you can develop a deep prayer life "on the run." (At least, thirty minutes to an hour is a good suggestion for a vibrant daily prayer life.) Remember, the only way we learn to pray is to "show up for practice." If you will spend significant time alone with Jesus, He will completely change your life!

Of course, we also embrace the glorious lifestyle of "prayer without ceasing" (1 Thessalonians 5:17). In other words, we learn to live every moment in the immediate awareness of God. Though we must be very committed to closet prayer time, we should never approach it as a legalistic bondage.

2. Approach your prayer time as a love relationship with God, not some legalistic ritual.

True prayer is a relationship! It is not certain formulas or programs. It is a love relationship with your God. *To view your prayer time as anything less is to miss the whole point of prayer.* More than anything else, God wants your love and this means making significant time to be alone with Him. We need to reflect on the biblical story of Martha and Mary (Luke 10:38-42). Many are so busy serving God that we neglect time alone with Him. This inevitably stunts our growth and short-circuits our power.

When you approach prayer as a relationship, you will also learn to hear God's voice on a daily basis. Not only will you be talking to God, but He will be talking to you! After all, true prayer begins with "listening" to God. *Genuine prayer always begins in the heart and mind of God!* Prayer is not you trying to tell God what to do. It is discerning what God wants to do and aligning your prayers with His will. You only get such discernment by spending significant time in prayer and meditative listening. As you learn to listen, you are then sure that what you are asking is God's will.

To hear God's voice, it is important to devote part of your prayer time to intentional meditation and reflection. During your time of meditative listening, write down key Scriptures and impressions God reveals. This form of journalizing is invaluable to a powerful prayer life! In many ways, learning to *hear* God is the greatest secret of answered prayer! In 1 John 5:14-15(KJV), this truth is very clear. "*And this is the confidence that we have in Him, that, if we ask any thing according to His will, we know He hears us: and if we know that He hears us, whatsoever we ask, we know that we have the petitions that we desired of Him.*"

3. Make a commitment to a biblically balanced prayer life by regularly practicing the five essential types of prayer.

It is essential that our prayer life be far more than reciting a list of "needs and wants." God wants His children to consistently experience great depths of personal praise and worship. Furthermore, we must experience daily cleansing or we cannot maintain the power of the Holy Spirit. He also wants to deepen our daily petitions and intercession.

Without question, a vibrant relationship with Jesus *requires* a consistent practice of five basic types of prayer: *(1) Praise, thanksgiving and worship, (2) Thorough confession and repentance, (3) Biblical petition and supplication, (4) Intercession* and *(5) Meditative listening.* Obviously, you can only experience all these prayer types if you make significant daily time to be alone with God. (It is impossible to regularly experience all the types of prayer in only a two or three minute devotion.) But believer, do not despair!

Through God's grace, you *can* begin to experience all prayer types on a daily basis.

4. In your daily petitions, focus more on issues of personal character and holiness than on temporal needs.

It is tragic when our personal prayer life consists mainly of health, finances and other earthly issues. Though important, such issues are earth bound and temporary. God wants to focus most on that which is eternal and kingdom oriented. After all, God's great priority is to conform you to the image of Christ. (Romans 8:29) He is deeply concerned about filling your thoughts and attitudes with His presence and holy power. If you are daily transformed in true holiness, your prayer and personal soul winning will explode as a natural result. But you may well ask, "How can I effectively pray for such transformation in my own life?"

A powerful suggestion is to make the nine fruit of the Holy Spirit your daily personal prayer petition. (Galatians 5:22) The fruit of the Holy Spirit represent the very character and holiness of God Himself. As you daily ask God to fill you with each fruit, also ask Him to show you how you *don't* reflect that characteristic. When you thus pray the Word of God for your own life, He will miraculously transform every part of your being! As you are filled with these fruit, prayer and witnessing become as natural as breathing.

The specific characteristics of the Beatitudes also provide excellent personal petitions. (Matthew 5) God will further lead you to pray other biblical character words on a regular basis. Some examples of character words are: humility, zeal, discernment, wisdom, genuine worship, immovability, boldness, purity, proper motives, revelation, etc. Ask God to help you focus your personal petitions on character, purity and holiness. If you daily pray such prayers for your own heart, God will revolutionize your life!

5. In your daily intercession, focus more on issues of evangelism and missions than on earthly concerns.

It is tragic that so much intercession is focused mainly on health and other temporal issues. God's great priorities are the evangelization of the world and sweeping revival in the Church (Matthew 28:18). If these are God's main priorities, they should also be the primary focus of our intercession. God does incredible things when we focus our intercession on lost people, missions and revival! Yet, you may be wondering, *"How can I focus my intercession on God's great priorities?"* Listed below are six powerful strategies.

(a) Develop a prayer list of lost people and intercede for them daily.

(b) Develop a prayer list of the key leaders and ministry strategies of your church. Pray for them regularly.

(c) Compile a prayer list of key spiritual and government leaders. Pray for them regularly.

(d) Regularly pray for vital mission strategies of your association, state and denomination. (Updates are available from your state and national denomination.)

(e) Daily intercede for revival and spiritual awakening in your city and nation. In my book, *How to Develop A Powerful Prayer Life*, I list twelve biblical prayers to help you effectively intercede for America and the world. (See resource mentioned below.)

(f) For all the various prayer subjects, develop a schedule to pray for certain items on particular days of the week. Otherwise it could be overwhelming. *However, always remain sensitive to God's promptings.* Don't ever become enslaved to a set schedule!

Dear friend, please do not feel that a powerful prayer life is out of your reach. If you are willing, God will revolutionize your praying and thus your walk with Him. For practical help, I have written the companion book, *How to Develop a Powerful Prayer Life.* It is designed to walk you step by step in a dynamic personal relationship with Jesus Christ and is designed to work hand in hand with this resource. In a very simple yet thorough way, it takes believers into the depths of a personal relationship with Jesus. This companion prayer tool is also priced so pastors can easily afford to order it for their whole congregations.

As we conclude this book, you now have a powerful tool for deep daily cleansing and mountain-moving prayer. The need for daily cleansing and growth is not something you will ever *outgrow.* Don't let anything keep you from walking in full cleansing and dynamic prayer. No matter how weak you have been, you *can* become a powerful, biblical intercessor. If God is for you, who can be against you? And believe me, dear Christian, God *is* for you! (Romans 8:31)

Appendix A

God's Word to Loving Fellowship and Unity
"Recognizing Christ's All-Important Command!"

Proverbs 6:16 – "*These six things doth the Lord hate: yea, seven are an **abomination** unto Him: A proud look, a lying tongue, and hands that shed innocent blood, an heart that deviseth wicked imaginations, feet that be swift in running to mischief, a false witness that speaketh lies, **and he that soweth discord among brethren.**"*

Matthew 5:9 – *"Blessed are the peacemakers: for they shall be called the children of God."*

Matthew 5:23-24;6:14-15 – "*Therefore if thou bring they gift to the altar, and there rememberest that thy brother hath ought against thee: leave there thy gift before the altar, and go thy way; first be reconciled to thy brother, and then come and offer thy gift…For if you forgive men their trespasses, your heavenly Father will also forgive you: But if you forgive not men their trespasses, neither will your Father forgive your trespasses."*

Matthew 22:37-40 – "Jesus said unto him, 'Thou shalt love the Lord thy God with all thy heart, and with all thy soul, and with all thy mind. This is the first and great commandment. And the second is like unto it, Thou shalt love they neighbor as thyself. On these two commandments hang all the law and the prophets.'"

John 13:34-35 – "*A new commandment I give unto you, that you love one another; as I have loved you, that you also love one another. By this shall all men know that you are My disciples if you have love one to another.*"

John 17:20-22 – *"Neither pray I for these alone, but for them also which shall believe on Me through their word; That they all may be one as Thou, Father, art in Me, and I in Thee, that they also may be one in Us; that the world may believe that Thou hast sent Me. And the glory which Thou gavest Me I have given them; that they may be one, even as We are one."*

Acts 2:1,42-47 – *"And when the day of Pentecost was fully come, they were all with one accord in one place…And they continued steadfastly in the apostles' doctrine and fellowship, and in breaking of bread, and in prayers. And fear came upon every soul; and many wonders and signs were done by the apostles. And all that believed were together, and had all things common. And sold their possessions and goods, and parted them to all men, as every man had need. And they, continuing daily with one accord in the temple and breaking bread from house to house, did eat their meat with gladness and singleness of heart. Praising God, and having favor with all the people. And the Lord added to the church daily such as should be saved."*

Romans 12:9(a),16-18 – *"Let love be without dissimulation. Be of the same mind one toward another. Mind not high things, but condescend to men of low estate. Be not wise in your own conceits. Recompense to no man evil for evil. Provide things honest in the sight of all men. If it be possible, as much as lieth in you, live peaceably with all men."*

Romans 15:5-7 – *"Now the God of patience and consolation grant you to be likeminded one toward another according to Christ Jesus: That you may with one mind and one mouth glorify God, even the Father of our Lord Jesus Christ. Wherefore receive you one another, as Christ also received us to the glory of God."*

1 Corinthians 1:10 – "*Now I beseech you, brethren, by the name of our Lord Jesus Christ, that you all speak the same thing, and that there be no divisions among you; but that you be perfectly joined together in the same mind and in the same judgment.*"

1 Corinthians 3:1-3 – "*And I, brethren, could not speak unto you as unto spiritual, but as unto carnal, even as unto babes in Christ. I have fed you with milk, and not with meat: for hitherto you were not able to bear it, neither yet now are you able. For you are yet carnal: for whereas there is among you envying, and strife, and divisions, are you not carnal, and walk as men?*"

1 Corinthians 11:18,29-31 – "*For first of all, when you come together in the church, I hear that there be divisions among you; and I partly believe it. For he that eateth and drinketh unworthily, eateth and drinketh damnation to himself not discerning the Lord's body. For this cause many are weak and sickly among you, and many sleep. For if we would judge ourselves, we should not be judged.*"

1 Corinthians 13:4-8(a) – "*Love suffers long, and is kind, love envies not; love vaunts not itself, is not puffed up. Does not behave itself unseemly, seeks not her own, is not easily provoked, thinks no evil; Rejoices not in iniquity, but rejoices in the truth; bears all things, believes all things, hopes all things, endures all things. Love never fails.*"

Ephesians 4:3 – "*With all lowliness and meekness and longsuffering, forbearing one another in love; Endeavoring to keep the unity of the Spirit in the bond of peace.*"

Ephesians 4:29-32 – "*Do not let any unwholesome talk come out of your mouths, but only what is helpful for building others up according to their needs, that it may benefit those who listen. And do not grieve the Holy Spirit of God, with whom you were sealed for the day of redemption. Get rid of all bitterness, rage and anger, brawling and slander, along with every form of malice. Be kind and compassionate to one another, forgiving each other, just as in Christ God forgave you."*

Philippians 4:8 – *"Finally, brethren, whatsoever things are true, whatsoever things are honest, whatsoever things are just, whatsoever things are pure, whatsoever things are lovely, whatsoever things are of good report, if there be any virtue, and if there be any praise, think on these things."*

Colossians 3:8,12-15 – *"But now you also put off all these: anger, wrath, malice, blasphemy, filthy communication out of your mouth…Put on therefore, as the elect of God, holy and beloved, bowels of mercies, kindness, humbleness of mind, meekness, longsuffering; Forbearing one another and forgiving one another, if any man have a quarrel against any: even as Christ forgave you, so also do you. And above all these things put on love, which is the bond of perfectness. And let the peace of God rule in your hearts, to the which also you are called in one body; and be you thankful."*

1 Thessalonians 5:13(b)-15 – *"And be at peace among your-selves. Now we exhort you, brethren, warn them that are unruly, comfort the feebleminded, support the weak, be patient toward all men. See that none render evil for evil unto any man; but ever follow that which is good, both among yourselves, and to all men."*

Titus 3:10-11 – *"A man that is a slanderer after the first and second admonition reject; knowing that he that is such is subverted, and sinneth, being condemned of himself."*

James 3:2-18 – *"For in many things we offend all. If any man offend not in word, the same is a perfect man, and able also to bridle the whole body...Even so the tongue is a little member, and boasteth great things. Behold, how great a matter a little fire kindleth! And the tongue is a fire, a world of iniquity; so is the tongue among our members, that it defileth the whole body, and setteth on fire the course of nature; and it is set on fire of hell...Who is a wise man and endued with knowledge among you? Let him show out of a good conversation his works with meekness of wisdom. But if you have bitter envying and strife in your hearts, glory not, and lie not against the truth. This wisdom descendeth not from above, but is earthly sensual, devilish. For where envying and strife is, there is confusion and every evil work. But the wisdom that comes from above is first pure, then peaceable, gentle, and easy to be entreated, full of mercy and good fruits, without partiality, and without hypocrisy. And the fruit of righteousness is sown in peace of them that make peace."*

James 4:11-12 – "*Speak not evil one of another, brethren. He that speaketh evil of his brother, and judgeth his brother, speaketh evil of the law, and judgeth the law: but if thou judge the law, thou art not a doer of the law, but a judge. There is one lawgiver, who is able to save and to destroy: who art thou that judgest another?*"

James 5:9 – "*Grumble not one against another, brethren, lest you be condemned; behold, the judge standeth before the door.*"

1 Peter 1:22 – "*Seeing you have purified your souls in obeying the truth through the Spirit unto unfeigned love of the brethren, see that you love one another with a pure heart fervently.*"

1 Peter 4:8-9 – "*And above all things have fervent love among yourselves: for love shall cover the multitude of sins. Use hospitality one to another without grudging.*"

1 John 2:9-11 – "*He that saith he is in the light, and hateth his brother, is in darkness even until now. He that loveth his brother abideth in the light, and there is none occasion of stumbling in him. But he that hateth his brother is in darkness, and walketh in darkness and knoweth not whether he goeth, because that darkness hath blinded his eyes.*"

1 John 3:10-15 – "*In this the children of God are manifest, and the children of the devil: whosoever doeth not righteousness is not of God, neither he that loves not his brother. For this is the message that you heard from the beginning, that we should love one another…We know that we have passed from death unto life, because we love the brethren. He that loves not his brother abides in death. Whosoever hates his brother is a murderer: and you know that no murderer hath eternal life abiding in him.*"

1 John 4:7-8 – "*Beloved, let us love one another: for love is of God; and every one that loveth is born of God, and knoweth God. He that loveth not knoweth not God; for God is love.*"

The Biblical Commands of
Loving Respect for Christian Leaders

Psalm 105:15 – "*Touch not Mine anointed, and do My prophets no harm.*"

1 Corinthians 1:10 – "*I appeal to you, brothers, in the name of our Lord Jesus Christ, that all of you agree with one another*

> *so that there may be no divisions among you and that you may be perfectly united in mind and thought."*

Ephesians 4:2-3 – *"Be completely humble and gentle; be patient, bearing with one another in love. Endeavoring to keep the unity of the Spirit in the bond of peace."*

1 Thessalonians 5:12-13 – *"And we beseech you, brethren, recognize them which labor among you, and are over you in the Lord, and admonish you: and to esteem them very highly in love for their work's sake. And be at peace among yourselves."*

1 Timothy 5:17 – *"Let the elders that rule well be counted worthy of double honor, especially they who labor in the Word and doctrine."*

Hebrews 13:17 – *"Obey them that have the rule over you, and submit yourselves: for they watch for your souls, as they that must give an account, that they may do it with joy, and not with grief; for that is unprofitable for you."*

(All verses above are from the King James Version)

Appendix B

How to Be Certain of Your Salvation

If you have any doubt about your salvation, I have great news for you. God wants to remove your doubts and give you absolute certainty! Without question, God intends *all* believers to have deep assurance in their relationship to Him. The following Scriptures make this abundantly clear.

> *"These things have I written to you that believe on the name of the Son of God; that you may **know** that you have eternal life, and that you may believe on the name of the Son of God."* (1 John 5:13, KJV)

> *"The Spirit itself bears witness with our spirit, that we **are** the children of God."* (Romans 8:16, KJV)

> *"And this is the confidence that we have in Him, that, if we ask any thing according to His will, He heareth us; and if we know that He hears us, whatsoever we ask, we know that we have the petitions that we desired of Him."* (1 John 5:14-15, KJV)

> *"The Lord is not slack concerning His promise, as some men count slackness; but is long-suffering to us-ward, not willing that any should perish but that all should come to repentance."* (2 Peter 3:9, KJV)

Since God obviously wants His children to have assurance, why do so many have doubt? Though there are different reasons for this pattern, one of the most common is that people have simply never been saved. In fact, there is significant evidence today's Church contains unusually high numbers of lost members.

In the last several decades, it has been frighteningly easy to "join a church" without having a life-changing encounter with Jesus Christ. For this reason, many people now find themselves members of churches, yet without a saving encounter with Christ. You may be wondering, "But why is this so prevalent in the modern church?" The following section provides key insight.

Why Are There So Many Lost Church Members?

Four Societal Factors

Though I would never claim to have any idea what the percentage may be, we can safely assume lost church members are not uncommon. *"Many will say to Me in that day, 'Lord, Lord, have we not prophesied in Thy name? and in Thy name have cast out devils? and in Thy name done many wonderful works?' And then will I profess unto them, 'I never knew you; depart from Me, you that work iniquity."* (Matthew 7:21, KJV) In our text, Jesus stated many will be shocked to find themselves barred from heaven. He did not say some or a few, He said many. This clearly implies it will not be uncommon for religious people to be barred from entering heaven. Four factors give strong clues about the usually high incidence of lost church members in today's church.

(1) *Over the last forty years, there has been profound moral and spiritual decline.*

There is no doubt our society has experienced a shocking moral plunge. It is also true that many churches are increasingly affected by societal patterns. Historically, in times of such spiritual decline, strong conviction of sin and reverence for God tend to lessen. Evidence of deep repentance and godly sorrow are far less evident than in times of great spiritual awakening. During periods of moral decline, history reveals a rising number of church members who evidence no life-change whatsoever. (They don't hold rue to their professions.)

In 1 John 2:19, we likely find a likely clue as to the reason why more than half of America's church members never attend! *"They went out from us; for if they had been of us, they would no doubt have continued with us: but they went out, that they might be made manifest that they were not all of us."* (KJV)Though such members may have raised their hand in some meeting or signed a membership card, they manifested no repentance and often cannot be found even six months later.

(2) *Much modern preaching and evangelism has placed far less emphasis on repentance and surrender to the Lordship of Christ.*

Consequently, many people have treated Christ as cheap "fire-insurance" to keep them out of hell. In such shallow man-centered preaching, God is almost portrayed as man's servant who primarily exists to make us happy and fulfill all our desires.

Though perhaps unintentional, many preachers have so emphasized God's love that the message of His awesome holiness is virtually ignored. Many have failed to preach the full consequences of sin and judgment. Such shallow, unbiblical preaching is very different from that of the New Testament church. It's also very different from the preaching in the generations of sweeping spiritual awakenings. Under such "man-centered" preaching, it is frighteningly easy for people to join a church without experiencing the strong conviction that produces genuine conversion. (2 Corinthians 7:10) In many churches, there is little evidence of anything remotely resembling the deep conviction and godly sorrow that produces genuine repentance and salvation.

(3) *For much of the past century, church membership was the socially "proper" thing to do.* (Though this has begun to change dramatically over the past twenty years.)

When church membership is the norm, it can be easy for people to join without a deep personal commitment to Christ. In many denominations, people can join churches with little or no thought about a serious relationship with Jesus. Often, people are not even asked about their relationship with Christ.

(4) *Churches often fail to give effective biblical counseling and instantly receive those desiring membership.*

In far too many cases, candidates are instantly received on the mere *assumption* they have been born again. For this reason, modern churches have many members who joined the church, but never joined Christ. New members' names were put on a membership card, but no one ever counseled them toward a personal prayer of deep repentance and faith.

Considering these four factors, you can see how easily people could join a church without being saved. As you have read these factors, you may suspect it describes some of your own experience. In the following section, I list common statements of church members who later came to realize they were lost. At the time of their original decision, most of these dear people had no idea they were making a false profession. Only in retrospect did they realize why they had made an inadequate decision. *Pause now and ask God to reveal whether any of the following statements apply to you.*

Commonly Stated Reasons for False Professions of Faith

Peer pressure - "Many of my friends were getting saved, so I joined mainly to be part of the group."

Expectations of Others - "My family and friends wanted me to get saved, so I joined the church mainly to please them."

Social Reasons - "Many of my friends were members of the church, so I joined in order to be socially acceptable. To be a responsible member of the community, I felt I needed to be a church member."

Inadequate Understanding - "When I made my decision, I really didn't understand the gospel of grace. I didn't comprehend my total dependence on Christ's blood and His gift of salvation." (In retrospect, I realize I was still trying to "earn" God's acceptance.)

Insincere Commitment - "When I made a decision, I experienced no real conviction or repentance. Though I made a surface decision, there was no change of ownership in my life. Consequently, I did not experience the new birth and I didn't become a new creature in Christ."

Shallow, Man-centered Preaching - "For the most part, I heard preaching that was shallow and un-evangelistic. I mainly heard devotions and social lessons. The full gospel of Christ was not made clear to me and I basically joined because I thought it was expected."

Inadequate Decision Counseling - "I did not receive clear biblical counseling when I joined the church. No one asked me to personally pray and seek God for a life-changing encounter with Christ. Though I joined the church, I was never led to seek Christ through a personal prayer of surrender and faith."

From the above statements, it is clear people can join churches for many reasons besides being genuinely born again. So how can you tell for sure if *your* decision was genuine? It really isn't that difficult because the Bible gives clear indicators of true salvation.

Under the next heading, we will examine some biblical signs of true salvation. However, for sake of balance, let me clearly state that even true Christians have days when the signs are not so evident. Saved people do experience periods when God may seem distant. It is certainly not my purpose to try to scare Christians into believing they are lost. Yet, at the same time, you must take the biblical indicators of salvation very seriously. *According to God's Word, the following factors are generally real and present in the lives of all who are truly saved.* Ask God to give you discernment as you prayerfully examine your life in light of His holy Word.

Essential Biblical Indicators of Salvation

1. **Genuine Christians can testify to a real and personal relationship with Christ.** *"And this is life eternal that they might know Thee the only true God, and Jesus Christ whom Thou hast sent."* (John 17:3, KJV) True salvation is far more than mentally believing certain facts "about" God. It is actually "knowing" God in a life-changing personal relationship. Jesus Christ is real to saved people; to them, He is more than a doctrine or mental belief. Tragically many people will miss heaven by about eighteen inches. (The distance between head and heart knowledge.)

2. **Saved people have experienced genuine conviction of sin and trust Christ alone for eternal life.** *"And when He is come, He will reprove the world of sin and of righteousness, and of judgment."* (John 16:8, KJV) *"For by grace are you saved through faith; and that not of yourselves: it is the gift of God."* (Ephesians 2:8, KJV)

   No one is saved by mere intellect. Neither can anyone be saved by just being in church or around Christian people. No one is saved by being a good person. You must be personally convicted of sin and drawn to Christ by the Holy Spirit. (John 6:44) There must be a time when you personally prayed and trusted Christ as your own Lord and Savior. Saved persons can readily testify to this reality in their lives.

3. **Genuine Christians possess a supernatural assurance they are saved and forgiven of their sins.** *"The Spirit itself bears witness with our spirit, that we are the children of God."* (Romans 8:16, KJV) This does not mean you never have any doubt, but it does mean a prevailing

peace will overshadow any momentary doubts.

4. **Children of God exhibit a hunger for spiritual growth and a genuine desire to turn from sin.** *"And every man that hath this hope in him purifies himself, even as He is pure."* (1 John 3:3, KJV) *"Whosoever is born of God does not commit sin; for His seed remains in him; and he cannot sin, because he is born of God."* (1 John 3:9, KJV)

5. **Genuine Christians sense God's real presence and hear His voice in their life.** *"My sheep hear My voice and I know them, and they follow Me."* (John 10:27, KJV) Because salvation is a personal relationship, true believers consistently experience the voice of Christ in their life. Friend, if God never speaks to your heart, you have reason for deep concern. If you have no desire for prayer and the Bible makes little sense to you, it is very possible you don't know the Savior.

6. **True Christians have a love for the Church and the people of God.** *"We know that we have passed from death unto life, because we love the brethren. He that loves not his brother abides in death."* (1 John 3:14, KJV) Perhaps the greatest mark of a saved person is a loving, compassionate spirit. If you have a consistently angry, unloving spirit, this is strong reason for concern. Furthermore, if you consistently lack the desire to worship and be around God's people, there is strong reason to question your salvation. (1 John 2:19)

7. **Most saved people can describe a "before and after" in terms of their salvation.** *"If any man be in Christ, he is a new creature: old things are passed away; behold, all things are become new."* (2 Corinthians 5:17, KJV) In the case of younger children, the sense of life transformation

may not be as pronounced, although some changes will be apparent even in children. To be born again is the most powerful transformation in human experience. Put simply, it is very doubtful that old things could pass away and all things become new and you somehow not know it!

After reading the biblical indicators of salvation, you may sense you are indeed saved, but at times still struggle with nagging doubts. Are there other sources of doubt besides being lost? The answer is yes. Under the next heading, I briefly describe three possible sources of doubt. We will address them one at a time.

Three Possible Sources of Doubt

If you are experiencing doubts about your salvation, there are at least three possible sources.

(1) *You may be saved, but have grown spiritually cold and backslidden.* It's possible you were never discipled or taught how to walk daily in the fullness of God's Spirit. As a result, you may have experienced little spiritual growth and are living in a perpetual state of quenching God's Spirit. If God's Spirit is quenched and grieved in your life, you will certainly lack the fullness of His Spirit and may often lack the feeling of His presence. It is possible you are saved, but in need of the daily cleansing and filling work of the Holy Spirit. If that is your case, working through the book, *Returning to Holiness*, will produce a glorious remedy for your doubts!

(2) *You may be saved, but Satan is constantly accusing and creating doubt.* (Revelation 12:10) If Satan can keep

you in doubt, your spiritual growth will be stunted and your service to Christ limited. You may be saved, but simply need to learn how to stand on God's promises and effectively resist the enemy. Our spiritual warfare is definitely real! In later paragraphs, I will give you an effective strategy for overcoming this type of spiritual oppression.

(3) *You may indeed be among thousands of lost church members who unwittingly made a profession that simply wasn't real.* (Matthew 7:21-24) In most cases, this was wholly unintentional. You certainly didn't mean to make a false profession but for a variety of reasons, you sense you have. For whatever reason, you find you are a church member with no peace about your salvation. Recently, I have seen several deacons, teachers and even pastors come to this realization and get saved. In every case, they came to a glorious new assurance and changed life. My friend, you can too!

So How Can I Know Christ in Perfect Assurance?

I ask you to set aside the next several moments and get utterly quiet before God. Claim God's wonderful promise from James 4:8. *"Draw near to God, and He will draw near to you."* (KJV) Ask God to draw near and clearly speak to your heart.

As you now draw near, purposely center your thoughts on God. Be assured, He is indeed with you this very moment. *Reflect on the glorious fact that God wants you to be saved and certain even more than you do!* Be assured, God is not playing hide and seek with you. He wants you to know

Him! Meditate on the glorious fact that Almighty God is very near to you this very moment.

You now need God's wisdom concerning the source of your doubts. You need to *know* for certain where you stand with Him. Pause in prayer and claim the following promise for wisdom. *"If any of you lack wisdom, let him ask of God, that giveth to all men liberally, and upbraideth not; and it shall be given him."* (James 1:5, KJV) God wants to give you wisdom concerning the source of your doubts.

Now turn back and prayerfully read the seven indicators of true salvation. If in the depth of your heart you sense you are saved but have merely lost God's fullness, then thank Him for your salvation. You should then return to page 23 and work through all the cleansing Scriptures in this resource. As you confess your sins and claim God's filling, you will rediscover the assurance and joy of your salvation. Your doubts will melt as you are increasingly filled with God's Spirit! (I also suggest that you read "The Illustration of the Wooden Stake" on page 168.)

If in the depths of your heart, you doubt you are saved, then thank God for the fact He has opened your eyes. It is certainly no "accident" you are reading this chapter. God has spoken to you for one reason — so that you can be saved and know it! It's time for your doubts to leave.

My friend, you will find peace when you learn trust God's infallible Word and not your own feelings. Your salvation does not depend on your feelings, but on Christ's unfailing grace and power. Because your salvation is based on God's own Word, carefully read the following Scriptures.

1. **God loves you and wants you to be saved.** John 3:16
   – *"For God so loved the world, He gave His only begotten*

Son, that whosoever believeth in Him should not perish but have eternal life." (KJV) Dear reader, place your name in that verse. Put your name in the place of the words *world* and *whosoever*. Now I want you to read that verse with your name in it. Read it slowly with your name in it. Read it out loud at least three times.

2. **Jesus took all your guilt and paid your penalty for sin.** Isaiah 53:6 – "*All we like sheep have gone astray: we have turned every one to his own way; and the Lord has laid on Him the iniquity of us all*" and Romans 5:8 – "*But God commendeth His love toward us, in that, while we were yet sinners, Christ died for us.*" (both verses KJV) My friend, God took **all** your sins and placed them on Jesus. He took the full penalty and death for all your sins (past, present and future). If you now receive Jesus' forgiveness, there is absolutely nothing left for which God could condemn you! Jesus has already paid your *entire* debt.

3. **God Himself is giving you the genuine desire to come to Jesus.** John 6:44(a) – "*No man can come to Me, except the Father which hath sent Me draw him.*" (KJV) The very fact you are reading this book and have a deep desire to know Christ is good indication God is drawing you to Jesus. Friend, if you truly desire to give your life to Jesus, rest assured God gave you that desire. Remember, God wants to save you even more than you want to be saved!

4. **Jesus receives all who sincerely come to Him in faith and repentance.** John 6:37 – "*All that the Father gives Me shall come to Me; and him that comes to Me I will in no wise cast out.*" (KJV) Please hear the certainty in Jesus' promise to receive you. In essence, He is saying, "There

is no way I will turn away those who sincerely come to Me." By His own infallible promise, Jesus promises to answer your prayer for salvation. God cannot lie! He is not playing cosmic hide and seek with those who come to Him. If you sincerely come to Him, He promised to receive you! (Romans 10:13, KJV *"For whosoever shall call upon the name of the Lord shall be saved."*)

5. **You must by faith receive eternal life as a free gift of God's grace.** Romans 6:23 KJV – *"For the wages of sin is death; but the gift of God is eternal life through Jesus Christ our Lord."* Ephesians 2:8 KJV – *"For by grace are you saved through faith; and that not of yourselves: it is the gift of God, not of works, lest any man should boast."* Salvation is a **gift** that we could never earn or deserve. We receive eternal life by simple child-like faith, not through human efforts to be good. "All our righteousness are as filthy rags." (Isaiah 64:6, KJV) There is absolutely nothing you could ever do to "deserve" God's forgiveness and salvation.

6. **God will give you a new heart and the grace to change.** 2 Corinthians 5:17 KJV – *"Therefore if any man be in Christ, he is a new creature: old things are passed away; behold, all things are become new."* Dear reader, you don't have to wonder, "Can I change?" Remember, it is God that changes you, not you that changes yourself. There is no one so bad that God cannot grant a brand new heart when they sincerely turn to Him. Do not make the tragic mistake of waiting until you think you can "fix" your own life before coming to Jesus. (That is a clever lie of Satan to keep you lost.)

7. **You must be willing to repent of sin and surrender your entire life to Jesus.** Luke 13:3 KJV – *"I tell you, no; but, except you repent, you shall all likewise perish."* I want to stress that repentance is not some human effort that *earns* salvation; for we are saved by grace through faith alone. (Ephesians 2:8; Titus 3:5) Salvation is all of grace and none of works (Romans 9:11). However, when you have saving faith, it means you recognize the Lordship of Jesus and are willing to surrender to His direction. You are willing (in reliance on His help) to transfer your life to His ownership.

Salvation doesn't mean you must somehow become perfect and never sin again, but it does mean a deep willingness to turn from known sin and follow Him. Salvation is a deep commitment of your life to Jesus, not some cheap ticket to heaven and a license to sin. But friend, no matter how weak you may feel, if you come to Jesus you will receive the grace to change! (John 1:12 KJV – *"But as many as received Him, to them gave He power to become the sons of God, even to them that believe on His name."*) When you receive Jesus, you get the power to change!

If you truly believe the seven truths stated above, please read the following sentences and place a check beside each statement.

☐ I believe Jesus Christ is the only begotten Son of God and died for the sins of the world.

☐ I believe God loves me and gave His Son to secure my salvation.

☐ I believe Jesus took my sins on Himself, paid sin's penalty, died a sacrificial death to remove my guilt and is resurrected at the right hand of God.

❏ I am deeply sorry for my sins that cost the death of God's own Son.

❏ I believe Jesus is the King of Kings and worthy of my full surrender and life-long obedience.

❏ I believe God's Spirit has opened my eyes and is drawing me to true salvation.

❏ I believe if I sincerely ask Jesus to forgive and save me, He will answer my prayer.

❏ I realize surrendering to Jesus means I will repent of sinful habits or relationships in my life.

❏ By depending on God's enabling grace and strength, I am truly willing to turn from my sins and surrender to Christ's Lordship.

❏ I desire to trust Jesus as my personal Lord and Savior right now.

Dear friend, if you could check off all the above statements, then according to God's promise, nothing in heaven and earth can keep you from being saved! (Romans 10:3) I'm going to ask you to pray the following prayer. I encourage you to *pause* after each sentence and let it sink in. You may even want to *repeat* each sentence to emphasize your sincerity. From your heart, tell God these or similar words. And remember the glorious promise of Jesus, *"Whosoever comes to Me, I will in no wise cast out!"* (John 6:37, KJV)

"God, I know I am a sinner and deserve eternal death —— I realize I can do nothing to save myself —— Dear Lord, I believe You gave Your Son to forgive and save me —— I am truly sorry for my sins —— By Your grace and help, I

now turn from my sins —— Jesus, please forgive me and come into my heart right now —— I trust You to be the Lord and Savior of my life —— Both now and forever, I surrender myself to obey You —— Help me fully live for You and serve You from this day forward —— Dear Lord, thank You for the grace and strength to turn from my sins —— Thank You for Your promise of eternal life ——In Jesus mighty name, I pray — Amen"

Date and Time Prayed:_____

Signed: _____

Dear reader, if you sincerely gave your life to Jesus, you will begin to sense the fruit of a changed life. (Romans 10:13) Do not overly concern yourself with what you feel or don't feel immediately. We are saved by faith in *Him*, not faith in our feelings.

On the spaces above, I encourage you to sign and date the time you prayed this life-surrendering prayer to God. Your written signature will become a powerful point of faith should Satan whisper doubts in the future. The following illustration provides a helpful strategy for overcoming future accusations or doubts.

The Illustration of the Wooden Stake

Our story is about a believer who had periodic doubts about his salvation. The man was genuinely saved but experienced occasional times of condemnation and doubt. When he had an especially difficult battle with temptation, he tended to doubt his salvation.

One day God gave him an idea that completely changed his life. He took a big wooden stake and, along with his Bible, went behind his barn. He opened the Bible to the promises of John 3:16 and Romans 10:13. He then knelt down and prayed a salvation prayer. He told God he was claiming His promise of eternal life. He sincerely asked Jesus to be his own Lord and Savior. After this simple heart-felt prayer, he drove the wooden stake deep into the ground with a little of the top left showing.

From that day forward, when he had struggles or doubts, he walked right back to that old stake and reminded himself of God's faithfulness. After talking to God, he usually said something like this: "*Right there by that stake, I know I called on the name of the Lord. Because God cannot lie, I know He heard me and I am His child!*" He then would say, "*Satan you're a liar and in Jesus name, I command you to flee!*" It wasn't long until Satan didn't bother to whisper any more doubts about his salvation. The man soon learned to trust God's Word, and not his own feelings or imperfect performance.

Do you now see the glorious key? We stand in *Jesus'* blood and righteousness, not our own. We trust in *God's* promise, not our feelings or performance. We trust in *God's* mighty grace to save and keep us, not our ability to deserve it. We trust in God's perfect faithfulness to us, not our imperfect faithfulness to Him. Do you see it, dear friend? Your security is in a grace that is greater than *all* your sin. So go ahead, child of God, **rest in Him**! And shout it from the housetops, "He is my Lord and Savior!" By the grace and blood of Jesus Christ, I *am* God's child!

So Where Do I Go From Here?

Jesus clearly said we are to *confess* Him before men. (Mark 8:38) For this reason, it is vital to let others know of the decision you just made. What just happened is the *beginning* of your walk with God. You now have the power to grow and develop into a mature child of God. However, growth will not occur by accident and it is crucial for you to get in a discipleship group. The first three commands for a new believer are as follows: (1) believer's baptism and (2) confessing Christ before people (usually in a local church) (3) becoming an active member of a local church (if you're not already). Your pastor will provide materials to aid in your growth as a new Christian.

At this point many ask, "*What about being re-baptized?*" Concerning this, your pastor should give you the primary guidance. However, I find the following simple principle to be helpful. *If you have a strong sense you were not saved when you were previously baptized, then baptism is definitely in order.* It is vital that you not allow pride to keep you from confessing and being baptized. (I have often seen one person's public profession cause many other lost church members to come under conviction and be saved!)

If however, you believe you really were saved and you just prayed to "drive down the stake of assurance," you and your pastor will decide the best course. You should definitely share your new assurance with the congregation. In any case, I strongly urge you to get the counsel of your pastor. Now go forth and live your life in the peace of God's glorious grace and endless love! Romans 8:1, KJV "*There is therefore now no condemnation to them which are in Christ Jesus, who walk not after the flesh, but after the Spirit.*"

Bibliography and Additional Resources

Adams, Jay E. *Sibling Rivalry in the Household of God*. Denver: Accent Books, 1988

Adams, Jay E. *Handbook on Church Discipline*. Grand Rapids: Zondervan, 1986

Adams, Jay E. *Marriage, Divorce, and Remarriage*. Grand Rapids: Zondervan, 1980

Baker, Don. *Beyond Forgiveness*. Portland: Multnomah Press, 1984

Bolton, Robert. *People Skills*. Touchstone, 1986

Buzzard, Lynn, and Thomas Brandon. *Church Discipline and the Courts*. Wheaton: Tyndale, 1987

Cosgrove, Charles H. and Dennis D. Hatfield. *Church Conflict: The Hidden System Behind the Fights*. Abingdon Press, 1994

Crabb, Lawrence J and Larry Crabb. *Connecting*. W. Publishing Group, 1997

Dobsen, Edward A., Speed B. Leas, and Marshall Shelley. *Mastering Conflict and Controversy*. Portland: Mulmomah Press. 1992

Fenton, Horace L., Jr. *When Christians Clash*. Downers Grove, IL: InterVarsity Press. 1987

Flynn, Leslie B. *When the Saints Come Storming In*. Wheaton: Victor Books. 1988

Frizzell, Gregory R. *Returning to Holiness*. Memphis: Master Design Ministries, 2000

Frizzell, Gregory R. *How to Develop A Powerful Prayer Life*. Memphis: Master Design Ministries, 1999

Gage, Ken and Joy. *Restoring Fellowship*. Chicago: Moody Press, 1984

Gangel, Kenneth O., and Samuel L. Canine. *Communication and Conflict Management in Churches and Christian Organization*. Nashville: Broadman Press. 1991

Halverstadt, Hugh R. *Managing Church Conflict*. Westminster John Knox Press, 1992

Haugk, Kenneth C. *Antagonists in the Church*. Minneapolis: Augsburg. 1988

Huttenlocker, Keith. *Conflict and Caring*. Grand Rapids: Zondervan, 1988

Kniskern J., Warren. *Courting Disaster*. Nashville: Broadman and Holman. 1995

MacNair, Donald J. *Restoration God's Way*. Philadelphia: Great Commissions Publications, 1978

Martin, Frank. *War in the Pews*. Downers Grove, IL: Inter-Varsity Press, 1995

McIntosh, Gary L., Samuel D. Rima. *Overcoming the Dark Side of Leadership: The Paradox of Personal Dysfunction*. Grand Rapids: Baker Books, 1998

Rediger, G. Lloyd. *Clergy Killers: Guidance for Pastors and Congregations Under Attack*. Westminster John Knox Press, 1997

Sande, Ken. *The Peacemaker*. Grand Rapids: Baker Books, 1991

Shelley, Marshall. *Well-Intentioned Dragons: Ministering to Problem People in the Church*. Bloomington: Bethany House Publishers

Thomas, Marlin E. *Resolving Disputes in Christian Groups*. Winnipeg: Windflower Communications, 1994

Van Yperen, Jim. *Making Peace: A Guide to Overcoming Church Conflict*. Chicago: Moody Press, 2002

Wecks, John. *Free to Disagree*. Grand Rapids: Kregel Resources, 1996

White, John and Ken Blue. *Healing the Wounded*. Downers Grove, Ill,: InterVarsity Press, 1985

Bibliographies on Assurance of Salvation Resources

Barna, George. *What Americans Believe*. Ventura: Regal, 1991

Beeke, Joel R. *Assurance of Faith*. New York, NY: Peter Land, 1991

Comfort, Ray. Hell's Best Kept Secret. New Kensington, PA: Whitaker House, 1989

deWitt, John Richard. *Doubt and Assurance*. Grand Rapids, MI: Baker, 1993

MacArthur, John. *Faith Works*. Dallas, TX: Word, 1993

MacArthur, John, Jr., *Saved Without a Doubt*. Wheaton, IL: Victor, 1992

Owen, John. *The Works of John Owen*. London: Johnstone and Hunter, 1850-53

Packer, J. I. *A Quest for Godliness*. Wheaton, IL; Crossway, 1990

Prange, Gordon W. *At Dawn We Slept*. New York, NY: Penguin Books, 1981

Prime, Samuel. *The Power of Prayer*. Edinburgh: The Banner of Truth Trust, 1992

Spurgeon, C.H. *Assurance Sought*. London: Passmore and Alabaster, 1917

Spurgeon, C. H. *Autobiography, Volume 2.* Edinburgh: The Banner of Truth Trust, 1973

Spurgeon, C. H. *I Know That My Redeemer Liveth.* London: Passmore and Alabaster, 1864

Spurgeon, C. H. *The Blessing of Full Assurance.* London: Passmore and Alabaster, 1889

Spurgeon, C. H. *Rest as a Test.* London: Passmore and Alabaster, 1901

Whitney, Donald S. *Spiritual Disciplines for the Christian Life.* Colorado Springs, CO: NavPress, 1991

Whitney, Donald S. *How Can I Be Sure I'm a Christian?* Colorado Springs, CO: NavPress, 1994

SDG